UnFunkt™

Quiet the Noise. Ignite the Light.

Jaime Marco

ISBN 979-89937811-0-5

UnFunkt™ is a trademark of Evolve Business Consulting, LLC

Cover and interior design by Keri Langlois

"The funk wants you distracted.

The world wants you busy.

But your people?

They just want you.

Fully present. Fully real."

– Jaime Marco

The People Behind the Pages

This book wouldn't exist without the people who lit the path before I even knew where I was going. While many have shaped this journey, I have to begin with one of the first.

To the late Professor, Jeff Butler, thank you for planting the seed. Your Human Relations class at the University of Central Florida was the first time I remember truly thinking about the power of human connection. Though you are no longer here, your influence lives on. You didn't just teach a course, you changed my course.

To the teams I've trained, the leaders I've coached, the audiences to which I have spoken, and the clients who let me walk alongside them, you brought this book to life. Your real-world challenges and real-time growth shaped every page.

To the friends (my BOD) who heard me say "I think I'm going to write a book" more times than any human should have to, thank you for listening to me, encouraging me, and never making me feel like I was dreaming too big. Thank you for being my sounding board, my support system, and my people.

To my parents, thank you for believing in me before I even knew what I was becoming. You have taught me that leadership starts at home, with how we treat people, how we communicate, and how we love.

To my husband, David, thank you for holding space for my passion, my chaos, and my late-night brainstorms. Your steady presence and deep belief in me have kept me grounded in the moments that mattered most.

And to my daughter, this book, this mission, this message, it's all a reflection of what I hope for you. You are my why. Watching you lead with heart, with humor, and with curiosity, reminds me daily that the future is bright and bold. You have taught me just as much as I hope to teach you. Thank you for being my greatest inspiration.

Here's to the people who help us believe, even before the words are written. Because the best stories are built on connection and I'm lucky to have you in mine.

Before We Begin...

Words shape how we see ourselves, our experiences, and our possibilities. So before we dive in, let's get on the same page, literally and figuratively. The following definitions aren't just clever wordplay (though, yes, UnFunkt™ is fun to say), they're the heart of this book. You'll see them woven throughout these pages as we explore the power of small, intentional actions to shake off what's holding you back and help you live, feel, and show up like you again.

UnFunkt™

adjective

/ˌənˈfəŋkt/ or uhn-FUNK't

The state of feeling fully you again; clear, confident, and reconnected to your spark after shedding the weight, fog, and funk of the world. When your energy is light, your purpose is loud and your presence feels like home.

Funk

noun

That heavy, hazy, stuck-in-the-mud feeling that sneaks in when life piles on too much noise, stress, or disconnection. It might show up as burnout, self-doubt, frustration, numbness or just not feeling like you.

It's not a failure. It's a signal.

Shedding the Funk

verb phrase

The intentional act of letting go of what's weighing you down physically, mentally, emotionally, or energetically. It's that moment you say: "Not today, funk."

Micro-Moves

noun

Small, intentional actions that create meaningful change. They are the seemingly tiny shifts in attitude, language, habits, or energy that stack up to create a big impact over time. They are a purposeful, repeated choice.

Hey you. Yeah, you. Before you dive in, you should know this book isn't a self-help cliché, it's not a productivity hack, and it's definitely not a "just manifest it!" pep talk in disguise.

This is a book about little moves.

The kind that shifts your mood, opens hearts, changes your day, and brings you back to yourself. You did read the definitions, right? If not, no judgment, so here it is again. "UnFunkt™" isn't just a fun word to say, it's a whole vibe. And *Micro-Moves?* They're the sneaky little power tools that get you there. So take what speaks to you, scribble in the margins, dog-ear your favorite pages, and try one little shift.

If you want to jot your thoughts, notes, or reflections right here on the page, go for it. If not, no worries. We've created two free companion tools so you can think, feel, scribble, and pause wherever works best for you (and keep your pages smudge-free if that's your thing).

The UnFunkt™ Companion Workbook
perfect for anyone ready to apply these moves to everyday life, relationships, and personal growth.

The UnFunkt™ Leadership Companion Workbook
designed for those in leadership roles who want to bring these moves into their teams, organizations, or communities.

Download Here   or   **Scan this QR Code**

www.jaimemarco.com/workbook

Choose the one that fits where you are now
or grab both and see how the moves can transform every area of your life.

Let's be real, most of us don't have time to read a book cover to cover. Good news; you don't have to. While every chapter builds toward something meaningful, *this* book is designed to meet you where you are.

It's a ***choose-your-now adventure*** because sometimes the shift you need most isn't on page one. It's on the page that calls to you when you flip it open. Follow your gut. Flip with purpose. Or just scroll through the Table of Contents and land where it feels right. Each UnFunkt™ Micro-Move includes a short description to help you quickly spot what might speak to you today. Trust your instincts. ***There's no wrong place to begin.***

And don't worry, at the end of each chapter, there is a suggestion of where to go next, whether it's a natural follow-up or a shift in focus.

You can always circle back later. This is your journey; your pace, your impact.

TABLE OF CONTENTS

This isn't just a book,

it's an intentional journey.

And the journey is yours

for the choosing.

I N T R O D U C T I O N

Before the Moves... Get in the Mindset

First, let's be honest.

Before we dive into the Micro-Moves that shift culture, confidence, and connection, let's talk about the space you're stepping into them from.

Because no strategy will stick if your head and heart are still stuck in survival mode. So before we "fix" anything, let's explore some things. Let's check in and see if this book is really for you.

Have you ever experienced something like this?

- *Burned out from trying to be everything for everyone.*
- *Quietly comparing yourself to people who seem to "have it together."*
- *Wondering if your energy even makes a difference anymore.*
- *Trying to lead while questioning if you're even doing it "right."*
- *Feeling invisible in a room full of people.*
- *Saying yes when you meant no, and resenting it later.*
- *Smiling through exhaustion because you didn't want to let anyone down.*
- *Trying to get through the day without losing your keys, your cool, or your calling.*

If even one of those made you say, "Yep, I've felt that..." Then *yes*; this book is for you.

It's not here to tell you to do more. It's here to help you do it differently.

To live with even more intention, not just endurance. To remind you that you don't have to earn your worth by over-functioning or over-extending. You just have to begin one small, brave move at a time.

Let's quiet the noise, the pressure, the performance.
Let's come back to what actually works, and who you actually are.

You're not behind; you are just starting from here. And that's exactly the right place to begin.

We're living in a world that's louder, faster, and more connected than ever, and yet we are somehow more disconnected than we have ever felt. The funk you feel? That foggy, frazzled, what-even-matters, energy? It doesn't happen in a vacuum.

It happens when we're over-informed but under-connected. Surrounded by people but starving for connection. No wonder so many people feel off, out of sync, or quietly running on empty.

Despite all our digital tools, disconnection is on the rise. In fact, a 2023 report from the U.S. Surgeon General found that nearly 50% of adults regularly report feeling lonely or isolated. That's despite being surrounded by apps, alerts, and endless streams of digital content. The study calls this a "public health crisis" because loneliness doesn't just impact our mental health, it affects our physical well-being, too.

Research at Harvard has found that genuine, in-person, connection remains the strongest predictor of overall life satisfaction.

Established in 2016, Harvard University's Human Flourishing Program aims to study and promote human flourishing by integrating knowledge from the empirical social sciences and the humanities. The program focuses on key aspects of well-being, including happiness and life satisfaction, physical and mental health, meaning and purpose, character and virtue, and close social relationships.

One of the program's significant initiatives is the Global Flourishing Study, a collaborative effort with Gallup and other institutions. This longitudinal study surveyed over 200,000 individuals across 22 countries to identify predictors and outcomes of human flourishing over time.

Findings from the study highlight that close social relationships are a central component of human flourishing. The quality of one's relationships has been shown to be a better predictor of long and happy lives than social class, IQ, or even genetics.

These insights underscore the profound impact of genuine, in-person connections on overall life satisfaction and well-being. It's not our productivity. Not our status. Not how "perfect" we appear online.

It's a connection.

And the problem? We often let perfection get in the way of connection. We filter. We polish. We overthink.

While we've never had more tools to communicate, many people report feeling more isolated than ever. According to Gallup's 2023 State of the Workplace report, only 2 in 10 U.S. employees strongly agree they have a best friend at work, and nearly 60% report feeling emotionally detached from their workplace.

And it's not just at work. A Pew Research study found that 8% of U.S. adults say they have no close friends at all, while over half have four or fewer. For men, the numbers are even more stark; the percentage of men reporting zero close friends has quintupled since 1990.

So despite living in the most connected era in history, we're often starved for real connection. Not pings. Not emojis. Not threads. Real, human connection the kind that makes us feel seen, supported, and like we belong.

We're communicating more, but connecting less. Most people work just steps away from their coworkers, but instead of turning their chair or walking down the hall, they'll send a text, a DM, or an email. Efficiency may be up, but the human moments? They are way down.

That disconnection deepened during the Covid pandemic when isolation became the norm and connection became a luxury. Sure, we gained flexibility, but we lost the little moments that used to glue teams together; spontaneous hallway chats, shared coffee breaks, the walk-and-talks between meetings.

In the years since, there has been an even bigger dramatic fallout. Many teams have found themselves physically back together but not always back in sync. The ripple effects of disconnection are still showing up. Teams are gathering in the same space, but not always connecting. People are clocked in but checked out. Rebuilding what was lost takes more than proximity; it takes intention.

This is where Micro-Moves matter most. Tiny, intentional moments of reconnection. The smile. The check-in. The pause. The "how are you really?" Because if we want our communities to thrive again, we have to stop assuming proximity equals connection and start building it, one small move at a time.

Connection isn't just about presence, it's about presence with purpose. It's about intentionally creating space for people to feel seen, valued, and safe to be real.

That's what fuels collaboration, engagement, and trust.

You don't need a title.
You don't need a perfect plan.
You don't even need a clue what's next.

You just need to be willing to believe that little moves can make a big impact, and you're already closer than you think.

Let's begin

This isn't just a book, it's an intentional journey.
And the journey is yours for the choosing.

This is actually more than just a book, it's a tool, a guide. A collection of small but mighty moves designed to help you make real change without turning your life upside down and get UnFunkt™.

If you're busy (who isn't?), overwhelmed, or honestly just don't know where to start, you're in the right place.

This book is for:

- *Someone who wants to grow and doesn't have hours to spare.*
- *Someone whose calendar is packed but still senses something needs to shift.*
- *Someone craving more connection, confidence, or clarity but doesn't want another self-help book that collects dust or guilt.*

You don't need more pressure. You need more practicality.

The self-help book shelf is crowded. You've probably seen a hundred of them. Maybe you've started a few. Maybe you even underlined some brilliant quote that now lives in your camera roll, somewhere between a screenshot of a recipe and a photo of your last vacation.

And yet, nothing really changed. That's because, if nothing changes, nothing changes.

Most books are written as though we've all got hours of uninterrupted reading time, no distractions, and a perfectly aligned morning routine. (Which, by the way, if you've figured out how to read, reflect, work out, meditate, journal, and drink lemon water before 8 AM, congrats. Please don't tell me – I'm fragile.)

Most of us are busy, stretched thin, and already trying our best. We don't need to be told to hustle harder. We need to learn what actually helps.

And here's the thing no one's really saying out loud; the way we live, work, and connect has changed. What made sense yesterday might not hold up tomorrow. The rules keep shifting, and the pressure to adapt is real.

But underneath all that change? What we really crave hasn't changed at all. We still want to feel seen. Heard. Connected. Like we matter and like what we do matters, too.

That's why I didn't write this book full of trendy advice or perfect-world solutions. I wrote it to be something that lasts. These Micro-Moves are small, yes, but they're foundational. To how we lead, how we live, and how we show up for ourselves and each other.

This isn't just a book for right now; it's a guide you'll come back to again and again, no matter what life throws your way.

When I decided to write this book I knew it had to be something real. Something human. Something that could help others. So I started paying even more attention to what people were saying, but also what they weren't saying.

Whenever someone asked for a recommendation and I suggested a book, the responses were almost always the same:

"I don't have time to read."

"Is there an audiobook?"

"I just want something I can actually use."

They weren't looking for theory; they were looking for traction.

Between work, family, relationships, calendars, and those mysterious 17 minutes a day we're supposed to spend stretching, it's a lot. So I wrote this book to fit real life. No guilt, no fluff, no need to read it all at once.

Recently, my dad joked about writing a book called "The Benefits of Low Goal Setting." And I've got to admit, I think he's onto something. Funny how the older we get, the wiser our parents seem to become. One minute we're rolling our eyes, the next we're quoting them. My dad's joke hit home because when everything feels like a lot, it's not the big leaps that change things, it's the little moves.

I started calling the small, intentional moves or shifts that fit into real life and actually stick, "Micro-Moves". They are not about changing everything overnight. They are about doing one small thing, purposefully, with consistency and letting that tiny move ripple out.

So that's what this book is about; 11 Micro-Moves that are grounded in behavior, backed by research, and inspired by real-life moments. I've seen them play out in both my personal and professional life. Each one of the 11 Micro-Moves are short to read, simple to try, and powerful in practice. You can try one a week, one a month, or one whenever you need to hit reset. You do you.

Now, you are probably asking, why 11? To me, 10 felt too expected and 11 is the number you choose when you know there's always room for one more move that matters. It's not just a number, it's a nudge. One more step, one more chance to move forward with intention. To me, 10 is a checklist, but 11 is a mindset. It's two ones side by side, reminding us that change isn't solo work, it's about showing up together. And maybe best of all, 11 is a mirror; one small move from which you can spark a big breakthrough in someone else.

Here's the extra spark: Each Micro-Move comes with its own Micro-Move reflection questions, a quick action step journal entry designed to help you pause, apply what you've learned, and actually do something with it. Because awareness is great, but action is what creates momentum.

And here's what makes this book even more personal; it is designed like a choose-your-own-adventure book (you are welcome, circa 1990). You don't have to read it straight through (unless you want to). The Table of Contents includes short prompts to help you decide where to begin based on what you're craving right now. Then, at the end of each reflection, you'll find a gentle nudge pointing you toward what to explore next depending on how you're feeling or what you're working through. Because growth isn't always linear, and life isn't one-size-fits-all.

What makes these moves even more powerful?
There's science behind them

Research shows that learning in small, focused bursts, which is called microlearning, improves attention, retention, and application. According to a study in the *Journal of Applied Psychology*, when content is broken into bite-size chunks and combined with reflection, learners retain 20% more and are significantly more likely to act on what they learn. And when people are given the autonomy to choose their own learning path, what to engage with and when, motivation and follow-through increase. Choice builds ownership. Relevance increases and the learning sticks longer, because it feels personal and self-directed rather than prescribed.

This reminds me of that old joke, "How do you eat an elephant? one bite at a time." But let's be honest, who wants to hurt an elephant? Or even think about eating one?

So what if we upgraded it? Forget elephants, let's snack our way through progress with a forkful of intention and a side of "you've got this."

Let's say: "How do you take on something big?" The answer? One Micro-Move, one brave step, one slightly chaotic, but totally worth-it, nibble at a time.

And there is even more research that supports the benefits of small intentional moves. Have you ever tried to learn something new, like an instrument, a dance, or something else?

Years ago I decided I wanted to teach myself how to play the guitar. To make it even more achievable, my sister bought me a guitar for my birthday because she believed in me. I even took a few lessons.

But here's where I went wrong. I tried to go pro by day three. I wanted instant fluency, instant rhythm, and instant crowd sing-alongs. And when that didn't happen? I got discouraged and I gave up.

Looking back, I realize exactly what I was missing; Micro-Moves.

If I had broken it down into tiny, manageable steps – one chord, one strum pattern, one simple goal – I could have stayed consistent. I could have felt progress instead of pressure. I didn't need to learn it all. I just needed to learn one move at a time.

That's the trap we all fall into – expecting ourselves to leap before we have even stretched. But the growth happens in the small moves, not the stage performance.

Turns out, learning something new isn't just humbling, it's also a reminder that progress doesn't come from cramming. It comes from showing up and learning, a little at a time. Which brings me to one of my favorite examples of Micro-Moves in action...

Micro-Moves in Action: Duolingo Gets It

The world's most popular language app, Duolingo, didn't succeed by asking people to study for hours. It succeeded by offering bite-sized, daily lessons that people could actually digest mentally. Each one takes about 5-10 minutes and builds slowly on the last, encouraging progress through consistency, not overwhelming the learner.

And the results speak for themselves. By mid-2025, Duolingo reported 130 million monthly active users, 47.7 million daily active users, and 10.9 million paying subscribers. That kind of sustained engagement isn't luck, it's proof that small, consistent actions work. Independent research by the City University of New York and the University of South Carolina found that just 34 hours on Duolingo equals an entire college semester of language instruction. Not because people crammed. But because they kept showing up in small, steady ways.

Their success is a masterclass in Micro-Moves; short, intentional actions that build confidence, capability, and momentum over time.

That's also what this book is about. No cramming required. So no, you don't have to finish this book in one sitting. You don't even have to start at the beginning.

Instead, flip to the Micro-Move that speaks to you. Try something new. Write something down. Say something out loud. Reflect. Repeat.

Because change doesn't require perfection. It just requires movement, tiny, intentional moves that add up over time.

Our Micro-Moves Matter Now More Than Ever

As previously mentioned, and certainly worth saying again so that it truly sticks, we live in the most connected time in human history: Snapchat, Instagram, Facebook, LinkedIn, text messages, DMs, Zoom meetings, and more, plus whatever new app just popped up this morning (Shmoozle? Yapper? ChatterSnap?). Ok, so I made those up but there's always another platform vying for our attention and they all come with notifications lighting up our devices like slot machines. They buzz, ping, and vibrate around us 24/7. All adding even more funk to our lives.

But here's the paradox; while we've never been so connected, we've never been more disconnected.

We're scrolling instead of speaking.
We're posting instead of pausing.
We're "liking" instead of listening.
We're commenting instead of connecting.

We're "on" all the time, but rarely present. And while our devices hum with activity, many of us feel like something is missing – a sense of meaning, community, alignment, and purpose. We're craving real connection. And not just with others but with ourselves.

It's time to get UnFunkt™. To come back to each other. To come back to presence, purpose, and impact. It's time to get back to humaning. And we do that one step at a time. Not through grand gestures or massive overhauls, but through something much more powerful, Micro-Moves. This book isn't just timely, it's necessary. Because we don't need more funk or noise, we need more meaning. And the way we get there isn't through a giant leap; it's through tiny, intentional shifts.

My obsession with people – why they do what they do, how they connect, and what makes them feel seen – started early. My parents always told me I was "gifted" (or maybe they said "fated") when it came to connecting with people. That instinct became more intentional when I took a Human Relations course with Dr. Jeff Butler at the University of Central Florida. In that class, we dove deep into the fascinating aspects of human behavior and connection and it opened my eyes to just how much relationships shape everything.

After graduating with a bachelor's degree in Interpersonal Communication from the University of Central Florida, I jumped straight into a dream job with Royal Caribbean Cruise Lines as Cruise Staff/Social Host. It was there somewhere between comedy shows, calling BINGO, teaching napkin folding, leading line dancing classes, and giving tips at international ports, that I fell deeper in love with understanding people. I watched how we all crave the same things; connection, appreciation, belonging, and how, no matter our background, the way we get there is more similar than we think. The thing that gets in the way? The funk.

The internal chatter. Overthinking. Trying too hard. The fear of not getting it perfect. So I made a choice – quiet the noise, and amplify the moves that actually create a powerful, lasting impact. And how? I'm sharing those moves with you. Because if even one of them helps someone feel more connected, more confident, more heard, then I'd scream it from the rooftops. (And for those of you that know me, you know I would.)

After more than 20 years of working in the leadership and empowerment space, I've learned something that shaped my entire career path – business doesn't run on strategies, systems, or spreadsheets, it runs on people. And people thrive when the human side of business is valued just as much as the operational side.

People often ask me, "Who's your ideal business partner? Who do you work with? Who do you serve?" My answer has always been the same – anyone with humans. That's why my career has taken me into such a wide range of settings; education, telecom, insurance, real estate, social networks, retailers, nonprofits, hospitality, and healthcare. Industries that couldn't look more different on paper, yet all share the same core truth – success depends on how well people connect, communicate, and collaborate.

I've kicked off the school year for teachers, spoken in auditoriums with over thousands of attendees, and worked with intimate executive teams around a single conference table. The size of the room or the industry doesn't matter; the human needs inside it do.

From workshops to keynotes, I've built frameworks that help teams lead, sell, and connect with their customers and each other even better. The Micro-Moves in this book are the high-level, accessible version of those deeper-dive frameworks I've refined over years in the field. Whether it's a sales team, a classroom, a call center, or a corporate boardroom, the principles of human connection don't just apply, they are what make everything else possible.

I can't tell you how many times after a keynote, workshop, or even a casual conversation, someone has pulled me aside and said, "I wish my boss could hear this." Or, "My sister needs this." Or, "I'm sending this to my kid's coach." It happens every time. Because these ideas aren't just relevant in one industry or one moment, they're human. This book is something people can hold in their hands, reflect on, share, and say, "This is what we've been missing." Because it's not about knowing everything, it's about doing small things that make a big difference.

And, it's not just about business. These same principles apply to personal relationships, because connection matters everywhere. If you love this for you, the kid version of the book is coming soon because big impact can start early. And for those who want to know exactly how these ideas apply in business, the UnFunked Leadership Companion Workbook will give you the tools to take them deeper into your teams and organizations.

"This isn't just a book,
it's a playbook for being human in a noisy world."

Then the rest flows

This book was born out of that truth; it is a practical, relatable guide to the real work of being human, on purpose and with purpose. Because when we choose the right Micro-Move at the right moment, we don't just improve our relationships, we improve our lives.

And that's exactly what this book helps you do. It's not just theory, it's action. It's not fluff, it's doable. And it's not about drastic change, it's about Micro-Moves. The kind you can make in the moment; the kind that actually sticks.

From cruise ships to classrooms, boardrooms to break rooms, sports fields to family dinner tables, it's how you show up that matters, your attitude, your presence, and the moments you choose to create. It's available to anyone willing to make the move. So no matter who you are – parent or coach, neighbor or new hire, student or CEO, teammate or teacher, sibling or friend – if you are a human who interacts with other humans, this book is for you.

You've probably heard the saying, "Attitude is everything." Well, as it turns out, that's more than just a motivational poster. Let's break it down.

If you assign a number to each letter in the word **ATTITUDE** based on its position in the alphabet, here's what you get:

A	**T**	**T**	**I**	**T**	**U**	**D**	**E**
1	20	20	9	20	21	4	5

Now add it all up: **1 + 20 + 20 + 9 + 20 + 21 + 4 + 5 = 100.**

That's right; attitude equals **100%.**

Now let's do the same thing with the words knowledge and hard work.

KNOWLEDGE: **11 + 14 + 15 + 23 + 12 + 5 + 4 + 7 + 5 = 96%**

HARD WORK: **8 + 1 + 18 + 4 + 23 + 15 + 18 + 11 = 98%**

Both are important, but they still fall short of 100%. Why? Because you can be the smartest person in the room, or the hardest worker on the team, and still miss the mark if your attitude sucks.

That's why these Micro-Moves matter. They're not about having all the answers or doing everything perfectly – they are everyday moves for anyone who wants to show up with an attitude of presence, curiosity, energy, and consistency. The kind of attitude that not only adds up to 100% but makes the people around you feel like they can give their 100% too.

This book isn't about perfection. It's not about being the loudest in the room. It's about learning how to be the clearest, the kindest, the most consistent. It's about tuning in to the moments that matter most and then choosing to act in ways that lift others and yourself.

In these pages, you'll find stories and real tools that can shift the way you connect, communicate, and show up in the world. Stop waiting for massive change. Start creating it with Micro-Moves. It's how you shed the funk, get UnFunkt™, and create an impact that doesn't just last, it multiplies. I call that the Butterfly Impact. It's inspired by the *Butterfly Effect* – the idea that even the smallest movement in one place can cause powerful shifts in another. When we show up with intention, we may be impacting people more than we will ever know.

The world doesn't need louder voices.
It needs clearer ones. Kinder ones. Human ones.

And the beautiful thing? You already have what it takes.
This isn't about becoming someone new; it's about remembering who you are.

Let's quiet the noise,
and choose presence over performance.

Let's tune back in,
and choose connection over perfection.

Let's create real authentic connection,
and genuine impact.

Let's get back to humaning.

And let's get UnFunkt™ one Micro-Move at a time...

How to Use This Book

Use this book as a space to reflect, write, reset, and apply what you're reading.

Research shows that when we think, write, and say our thoughts out loud, we activate multiple parts of the brain, reinforcing learning and increasing retention by up to 70% more than just reading or listening alone. In fact, the act of writing helps clarify intention. The act of speaking builds commitment, and together, they create transformation.

Now let's get started.

We're kicking things off with the kind of Micro-Move that makes a big impact. And that's what this book is all about, small, intentional actions that don't just shift your mindset or behavior in the moment, they create an impact. One shift in your tone, one moment of presence, one act of ownership and the people around you feel it.

Each chapter introduces one of these powerful Micro-Moves and every one of them comes with four components to help you take it further:

The WHAT

A simple description of the Micro-Move.

The WHY

The science behind the move – the research that shows why these small moves work.

The HOW

The social proof and real world ripple – a personal story or human moment that shows how it plays out in real life.

The NOW

Your Micro-Move reflection – a space for you to pause, apply, and take action.

Before we dive into the Micro-Moves, pause and reflect with the following questions so that you can start with clarity. Every little Micro-Move builds on your reflection response below. So take a minute; be honest. You don't need the "right" answer, just your truth. Your "why?"

Your Micro-Move
REFLECTION

Why did you pick up this book?

_____

_____

What's happening in your world that made you stop and say:
"It's time for a shift."
It doesn't have to be big, just real.

_____

_____

What would it feel like to show up as your best self more often?

_____

_____

Now visualize it.
A day where you felt proud, aligned, energized, connected.
What's different?

_____

_____

UnFunkt™

BRING THE VIBE

BE

THE VIBE

The vibe you bring

is the permission slip everyone

else feels to show up fully.

Bring the Vibe, Be the Vibe

Start Here. Always.

Because energy comes before everything else.

Before your words, your intentions, your ideas, your energy walks in first. It sets the tone. It shapes how you're received. It determines whether people lean in or tune out.

If you skip this step, the rest won't land the way you want it to. But when you get this right? Every move thereafter becomes more powerful, more connected, more you.

That's why this Micro-Move comes first. Because how you show up changes what happens next. Every time. We've all experienced it firsthand.

You walk into a room, and the mood shifts. You didn't say a word but your energy did.

We all bring energy into spaces. The question is: Are you aware of it?

Are you choosing it or just dragging it in from the last meeting, the traffic jam, the group chat, or the grocery line?

Your energy introduces you before your name ever does. Your tone, your posture, your eye contact, even the way you breathe, it all speaks before your words do. And, your energy, it's contagious. The only question is, what are people catching from you?

People often use "energy" and "attitude" interchangeably. But when we think in terms of "attitude," we usually reduce it to two options – positive or negative. That's too black or white.

Your energy isn't just about being "positive" or "negative." Such binary thinking oversimplifies something considerably more complex. Those words? They're vague. They're loaded with personal values. And they mean a million different things to a million different people.

Let me show you what I mean with one of my favorite quick exercises.

Whether I'm with a team of 23 or a crowd of 1,000, I ask everyone to define one simple word: **HOT.**

That's it. H-O-T.

Then I give them one minute to jot down every meaning, feeling, or image that comes to mind.

One tiny word, endless interpretations. Try it right now. On a scrap piece of paper, here or in your companion workbook, write down as many meanings for the word HOT as you can.

I've seen people come up with 5 meanings, 10 meanings, even 28 different meanings (shout out to that library team!).

Scan or download the workbook at **jaimemarco.com/workbook**

You might have written spicy, sexy, trendy, temperature or, if you're feeling edgy, maybe even stolen. But someone else? They might've gone with overheated, angry, on fire, taboo, bold, or even popular. Some might have leaned into humor, like jalapeño, burnt toast, or Paris Hilton, circa 2003. Some people say, "Hot like the weather in Florida in August, when your skin sticks to the car seat."

Someone always throws in, "Hot mess." Not sure if I should be offended at that point. They aren't wrong; aren't we all hot messes? Ok, back to the point.

One word, endless meanings. Some good, some bad, some totally neutral until you know the context. It always leads to a moment of realization in the room. If one little word like "hot" can mean so many different things, why do we assume words like "positive" or "negative" are any clearer?

That's the problem with trying to label energy as simply positive or negative. It's not just oversimplified, it's inaccurate. Because our definitions are shaped by experience, emotion, culture, even mood.

What seems like "positive energy" to you might feel "over the top" to someone else. What seems "negative" to one person might actually be calm, focused, or just quiet to another.

Energy isn't just what you have, it's what you bring. And the more intentional you are about it, the more power you have to shift a room for the better.

Your energy isn't about being upbeat or cheerful all the time. It's about being tuned in and aware enough to choose the right energy for the moment.

Sometimes that's grounded. Sometimes it's light. Sometimes it's fire.

Sometimes though, the real challenge isn't just choosing your energy, it's protecting it.

Here's what we don't talk about enough; there are energy givers and energy takers. Energy givers leave others feeling a little lighter, a little more hopeful, a little more alive. Energy takers? Well, they leave you feeling drained, second-guessing yourself, or like you need a nap and a snack just to recover.

One of the hardest life lessons to learn is this; you have to protect your energy. That means sometimes walking away from people, environments, or dynamics that drain you, no matter how much you care, how long you've known them, or how much potential you see in the relationship. If the input you're giving constantly outweighs the output you are receiving, you'll burn out. Even the sun has limits.

But the problem isn't always about your energy. Some people won't get your light. Some might even resent it. That's okay. Don't lower your frequency to match theirs. Don't dilute your joy, your passion, your boldness to be digestible for people who never really wanted to taste it in the first place.

Instead, find your people. The ones who see your energy and say, "Yes, more of that." The ones who not only appreciate what you bring to the table but bring their own dish too.

Bringing the vibe doesn't mean being "on" all the time. It means being intentional about how you show up and recognizing who's pouring into your cup versus who's poking holes in it.

That's why I am not advocating chasing constant positivity, I am simply suggesting choosing and protecting the right energy for the moment.

Instead of defaulting to positive or negative, be even more specific. Because the right energy is different in every moment.

It's not about "being positive." It's about being present enough to choose what the moment actually needs. The right energy equals the right attitude. It's not one-size-fits-all, it's moment-by-moment intentionality.

So instead of asking,
"Am I being positive enough?"

Try asking:
"Am I bringing the right energy for what this moment needs?"

That small shift changes everything. Because it's not about forcing a smile or pretending to be okay. It's about choosing to show up with intention.

Feeling overwhelmed? Maybe what's needed is calm focus, not forced cheer.

Helping your kid with homework? Bring patience and encouragement.

Talking to a friend who's having a rough day? Bring presence and softness.

Celebrating your partner's win (big or small)? Bring joy and real attention.

Setting a boundary with someone you love? Bring calm and clarity.

Dealing with a stranger who's rude? Bring grace or a deep breath and a clean exit.

There's no one-size-fits-all vibe.

There's just this moment and the energy you choose to bring to it. That's the real energy shift. It's not about putting on a happy face. It's about showing up with the energy that fits the moment and protects your own in the process.Because that's how real connection happens: not through perfection, but through presence.

The Science 🧠 Behind the Move

Science backs it up; your energy matters more than you think. Humans are wired to feel what others feel thanks to something called mirror neurons. These neurons don't just fire when you experience something, they also fire when you observe someone else. So when you walk into a room with anxiety, frustration, or warmth and calm, other people's brains actually pick up on it.

It's called "emotional contagion," and research from psychologists Hatfield, Cacioppo, and Rapson shows that our emotional states are highly contagious, even without words; we catch energy like a cold, good or bad.

According to research from the University of California, emotional contagion is a real, measurable phenomenon. When someone walks into a space with positive energy, confidence, calm, encouragement, those around them actually begin to mirror it neurologically.

Why? Because of those mirror neurons - the parts of our brain that help us connect and relate. That includes facial expressions, tone, and body language.

Translation: If you're rushed, irritable, or low-vibe, people don't just see it, they feel it. And it's not just personal, it's professional.

According to a joint study between *Harvard Business Review* and *The Energy Project,* how leaders manage their energy has a greater impact on employee engagement than any other leadership trait. Teams led by "energizing leaders" are more than 3 times as likely to be fully engaged.

Want to go deeper? A study from the University of Michigan found that teams who worked with "positive energizers" experienced:

Higher job satisfaction
Increased learning and innovation
Better collaboration and retention

And here's a favorite statistic that says it all: According to communication researcher, Dr. Albert Mehrabian, only 7% of your message comes from words. The rest?

38% tone. 55% body language.

So, your energy is your message. The way you carry yourself is likely to be remembered long after your words are forgotten. And it works the other way, too. When you're grounded, present, optimistic, and intentional, you raise the room without saying a word.

The Social Proof & Real World Ripple

Have you ever been desperate for peace only to have someone else's energy completely hijack the room?

I booked a spa day because I needed to reset mentally, emotionally, everything.

You know the kind of need I mean, when your shoulders are basically earrings and your brain won't stop sprinting.

I showed up early and melted into the waiting room's soft piano music and lavender mist. Everyone around me looked halfway to nap mode, including me.

And then, one by one, the massage therapists began to appear to come and collect their next client.

Each one moved like a deep breath. Calm energy. Soft voice. One gently extended her arms to her client and whispered, "Come with me, I'm here to help you relax."

I waited, eager, ready. So ready. And then mine walked in. Door swings open. Clipboard smacks. A loud voice echoes. "JAIME?" she barked.

Everyone looked up, including me – startled, tense, and already bracing.

My shoulders immediately returned to their permanent post near my ears. I stood up slowly, trying to hold onto any last thread of calm. She turned on her heel, barely making eye contact, and as we walked back, she asked, "How are you today?"

But not like a question. More like a formality. Like she had zero intention of listening to the answer.

And that's when it really landed; our energy walks in before we do. Our words follow close behind. And people can always tell the difference between saying something...and meaning it.

That moment became part of the reason I created my TEDx talk, "No More How Are You's" because too often, we ask questions to which we don't care to hear the answers. And connection deserves more than that.

My TEDx talk was built around this very concept of intentional connection. Back to the idea that the words we use shape the results we get. That talk wasn't just about a phrase, it was about how we show up, listen, and create real presence in a world full of noise.

One of the key Micro-Moves I shared is simple but powerful; we need to stop asking each other, "How are you?" It's one of the most commonly used questions in the world but is rarely genuine; it is said as a placeholder. A greeting. A default line we toss out in passing. And more often than not, the answer isn't honest. It's "good," "busy," "okay," "living the dream," or the dreaded four-letter F-word, **F.I.N.E.**

You know what that actually stands for?
Freaked out, **I**nsecure, **N**eurotic, and **E**motional.
We've all heard it. When someone says they're "fine," almost no one stops to check in further. No one asks what's behind it. So we walk away thinking we've connected, when really, we've just exchanged autopilot pleasantries.

Ask shallow questions, and you'll get surface-level answers and relationships. But shift the question, and you will shift the conversation.

That's why I've become known as the "No More How Are You's Girl," and it's why I challenge teams, leaders, and friends alike to change the question. Ask something real. Try:

"What's been the highlight of your day so far?"

"What's one word to describe your week?"

"What's something on your plate that I can support you with?"

Because connection isn't about being polite. It's about being present.

It's about seeing and hearing each other without the need to perform, impress, or polish.

So yes, one Micro-Move that makes a huge impact is ditching the "How are you?" and replacing it with something that creates space for truth, trust, and togetherness.

Sometimes, I'll even ask a different question entirely: "On a scale of 1 to 10, what's your number today?" One means you shouldn't be peopling (yep, I made that a verb), and 10 means it's the best day you've ever lived without a worry in the world.

Here's the fun part, regardless of the number someone gives, it's just a starting point; it opens the door to a real conversation. Sure, someone might say "10," but let's be honest, who really has zero worries? And if they say "3," I don't ask, "Why so low?" In fact, I never ask, "Why is that your number?" That can feel intrusive or put someone on the spot before they are ready to share.

Instead, I gently ask, "What would it take to move just .25 higher?" That small shift invites curiosity without pressure. It focuses on possibility rather than judgment and that's where real connection and progress begin.

That question does something beautiful. It shows that you're not asking them to leap or fake it, you're just offering space for possibility. For support. For a step.

The "What would it take to go .25 higher?" approach, or really, any intentional check-in that goes beyond the automatic "How are you?" creates genuine impact again and again.

One of my favorite examples happened in a parking lot.

My family was headed to a Tampa Bay Rays game. If you've ever been to a baseball stadium on a stormy day, you know the parking situation can be stressful. It was chaotic, raining, and we were just trying to get into the stadium as quickly as possible.

As we pulled up to the booth, a parking staffer leaned out with his scanner and said, "Welcome! How are you guys?" But you could tell he didn't really care how we were, he was just on autopilot. It was a reflex. A routine hello delivered out of habit, not intention.

That's when it happened. My husband was driving, and I gave him the stare. You know the one. The "you know what to do and I will elbow you if you don't" stare. I locked eyes with him and said, "Do it." He knew exactly what I meant. (Marriage – where entire conversations happen with eyebrows.) So instead of the usual "Good, how are you?" he replied:

"Hey, what's going to be the best part of your night?" And the guy stopped. He literally froze for a second and looked dumbfounded. Then he looked at us, smiled, and said, "You know what? No one has ever asked me that."

He went on to share that he had just started the role a few weeks earlier and he was excited to have the booth job because he would be covered during the storm. Then he said something that stuck with me: "Thanks for asking."

That moment didn't require a deep conversation, it just required a even better question. And in less than ten seconds, what we did made a difference, because for a split second, he felt seen, not as a ticket-taker, but as a human.

And sometimes, that's all someone needs to shift their whole day. And these moments? They don't just happen at ballparks or in big breakthrough conversations. They happen anywhere and everywhere, if you are open to them. This next one hit even harder.

Not long ago, I made a quick stop at one of the grocery stores in my area. It was one of those in-and-out missions, right when they opened at 7:00 a.m. I had just a few minutes before I needed to be back on the road for an appointment.

I was in a rush; it was early and I wasn't exactly in full "let's connect with humanity" mode. In fact, I was fully prepared to do very little peopling. But even in those moments, especially in those moments, I try to remind myself, my energy is contagious. And while I could have brought my chariot-of-chaos, coffee-fueled, spazz energy into that space, I didn't. Because I believe in the power of connection and I try to live out that value, even when I'm on a tight schedule.

So when the woman working the checkout area greeted me with the standard, "Good morning, how are you?" I didn't just mumble "good" and keep moving. Instead, I paused and asked: "Good morning, what's going to be the best part of your day today?" She stopped, surprised in the best way, and replied, "Actually, today is my one-year anniversary working here."

Naturally, I smiled and said, "Congratulations!" And then she added: "My husband passed away two months before I started." Reflexively, I said: "Oh my gosh, I'm so sorry." And without skipping a beat, she said: "Don't be sorry. I'm not." And that's when the story really unfolded.

She shared that for 17 years, she had been married to a man who didn't allow her to work. Didn't allow her to have friends. Didn't allow her to do anything on her own. This job, this anniversary, wasn't just a milestone, it was freedom. Reinvention; a new beginning. And in the middle of a grocery store, at 7:00 a.m., during a moment I could have missed if I wasn't intentional about my energy, we shared a hug, a laugh, and a story that mattered.

That's why I ask; that's why I pause. Because even when time is tight and life is loud, choosing intentional energy can change everything. And often times, all it takes is one unexpected question.

These Micro-Moves help us connect on a deeper level. They uncover stories, build trust, and remind us that life isn't about having all the answers. It's about creating moments of real connection.

What's even more fun is seeing how this little practice has taken on a life of its own. I've shared it with friends, colleagues, teachers, clients, even strangers on airplanes, and now I see it popping up everywhere. (I make friends everywhere. Shoutout to 13B, who left the flight with a new perspective and my LinkedIn profile.)

The best part? People have started "stealing" it (with love), making it their own, and weaving it into their lives in the most beautiful, creative ways. I've met families who start dinner by asking for everyone's "number." I've seen friend groups text it in the middle of a rough day "Hey, I'm at a 4.3... just FYI." And one of my personal favorites? Someone told me they leave a sticky note on the bathroom mirror with their number each morning so their partner knows where they're at, no explanation needed.

The point isn't the number. It's the invitation. It's a simple, playful, Micro-Move that opens the door to real talk, honest check-ins, and just a little more humanity in the middle of whatever chaos life's throwing at you. And here's the magic; whatever your number is, it's okay. It can shift. It can rise. It can dip. You're not stuck. What matters is creating space to name where you are so people can meet you there.

And here's the really important part: You don't have to be a 9 or 10 to show up.

You don't have to pretend. You don't have to power through. When you're honest about where you are, even if it's a 4.75, that's when real connection happens.

Because your truth gives other people permission to be real, too. And when we stop faking it, we start actually feeling it.

That's why this Micro-Move matters now more than ever. That's why we start here. Because it's not just about showing up, it's about the energy you bring when you do. Reconnection won't come from perfect schedules, motivational quotes, or curated posts; it comes from Micro-Moves.

From a person walking into the room with grounded, open energy.

From a friend texting "I'm a 6 today, but I'm trying."

From a sticky note on the fridge that says "Today I'm a 5.25" because even that says, "I'm here. I'm real."

These aren't just gestures; they are realignment cues. They help us reset the moment. They remind us we're human. And they bring us back to each other in the moments that matter.

REFLECTION

Bring the Vibe, Be the Vibe

Connection doesn't require performance; it requires presence. And presence begins with the energy you choose to bring.

Connection isn't just something you feel, it's something you create. Let's put that into motion:

1. Who in your life leaves you feeling more energized after spending time with them and who leaves you feeling drained?

_____

_____

_____

2. If others could describe your presence in one word, what would you hope they say? Is it the same energy you're currently giving?

_____

_____

_____

3. What's one question you could ask that opens the door to real conversation beyond "How are you?"
   (Think: "What's been the high point of your week so far?" or
   "What's something you're proud of today?")

_____

_____

_____

4. Use the "1 to 10" scale, what's your number today? What would make it go .25 higher?

_____

_____

_____

5. What boundaries or shifts might help you protect your energy while staying true to who you are?

_____

_____

_____

6. What's one small ritual or Micro-Move you can use to reset your energy throughout the day so you show up as the person you want to be, not just the person you feel like in the moment?

_____

_____

_____

CHOOSE YOUR NEXT MOVE

2 PAGE 17 ▶ If you're ready to keep building from here, turn the page to **Micro-Move #2: Pause with Purpose.**

But if today you're feeling...

4 PAGE 45 ▶ Like you're spiraling in self-comparison? Jump to **Micro-Move #4: Dare to Compare – Just Don't.**

Or feeling...

5 PAGE 59 ▶ Disconnected from those around you? **Flip to Micro-Move #5: Fuel Others with Appreciation.**

UnFunkt™

PAUSE WITH PURPOSE

Sometimes the most productive thing

you can do is nothing

for a moment, on purpose.

Pause with Purpose ;

Let's be real: most of us are moving too fast.
We rush from moment to moment, conversation to conversation, errand to errand, reacting instead of responding. And when we're stuck in go-mode, we miss the magic of the pause.

A purposeful pause doesn't mean doing nothing. It means doing something different. It means choosing to stop, breathe, and create space.

Space to think; space to feel; space to decide how you actually want to show up. One of the most powerful tools we have as humans, partners, parents, friends, strangers, is the ability to pause before reacting.

To pause:
Before sending that text.
Before snapping back.
Before spiraling into assumptions.
Before jumping to conclusions.

Power isn't found in urgency; it's found in intention. Pausing doesn't slow you down, it sets you up to move forward with clarity. It gives you the ability to lead with perspective instead of pressure. To respond instead of react; to choose the tone, the energy, the direction. In a world that rewards speed, the person who pauses stands out.

The pause helps you connect to your values; it helps you check your bias. It gives you a second to ask: "Is this how I want to be remembered at this moment?"

It's a Micro-Move with macro impact and the more you practice it, the more natural it becomes. Over time, the pause becomes a reflex, not a delay, but a decision point.

And in that space; that's where growth happens. That's where empathy sneaks in. That's where connection gets real.

We've all been there. Those moments when your heart races, your palms sweat, and your mouth opens before your brain catches up. That's what experts call an emotional hijack. It's when your amygdala, the part of your brain responsible for emotion, goes into overdrive, flooding your body with stress hormones before your logical thinking even has a chance to chime in. It's biology's version of pressing "send" on an email you definitely should have saved as a draft.

You know, that moment in a conversation when the words leave your mouth and you instantly think, " I would love to rewind time and not say that."

What tends to make these hijacks end in flames? The fact that we react before we pause. We let our feelings take the wheel before we've even buckled in our awareness.

That's why the pause is so powerful. It interrupts the emotional hijack. It creates a beat between the trigger and the reaction, a beat where choice can live. And that beat? That's where real human connection lives, too.

The Science Behind the Move

Studies show that when we take a moment to pause, just a breath or two, we activate the parasympathetic nervous system, which helps us calm down, refocus, and access better decision-making. According to a study published in *Harvard Business Review*, leaders who practiced mindfulness, even briefly, were more productive, less reactive, and better at leading under pressure.

In fact, the simple act of pausing has been linked to lower cortisol levels, improved memory recall, and better emotional regulation. Translation? A tiny pause can lead to better outcomes in just about every situation.

The Breathwork Behind the Pause

In yoga, there's a practice called Pranayama, the intentional control of the breath. Prana means life force; Yama means control. And the science backs what yogis have known for centuries; when we breathe on purpose, we lead on purpose.

Intentional breathwork activates the parasympathetic nervous system, our internal "reset switch." Which lowers stress hormones, slows the heart rate, and reopens access to the parts of our brain responsible for empathy, logic, and creativity.

Translation: A well-timed breath literally changes how we think and lead.

And it's not just yogis using it. One fundamental technique employed by SWAT teams, Navy SEALs, Olympic athletes, and high-pressure professionals, is the pause. They train in a technique called box-breathing, a structured breathing method that enhances focus and regulates stress responses. It helps them regulate their stress response in real time because composure is a performance edge.

What is Box Breathing?

Box-breathing, also known as four-square breathing, involves a simple pattern. ⟶

This cycle is repeated several times, promoting a state of calm and focus. Studies have shown that controlled breathing techniques like box-breathing can significantly reduce cortisol levels. Which leads to decreased anxiety and improved mood.

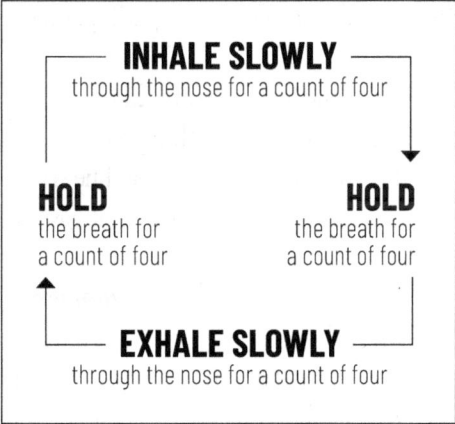

INHALE SLOWLY
through the nose for a count of four

HOLD
the breath for
a count of four

HOLD
the breath for
a count of four

EXHALE SLOWLY
through the nose for a count of four

Additionally, research also shows enhanced cognitive function and physiological benefits. Regular practice of box breathing has been associated with lowered heart rate and blood pressure, contributing to overall cardiovascular health.

When we talk about pausing with purpose, we're not just talking about taking a break. We're talking about regulating our internal system. We're choosing to slow down just long enough to shift from reaction to intention.

One breath, one beat, one ripple of calm in a room that desperately needs it.

When we pause, we give others permission to do the same. We model calm, we model clarity, we model intention. In a world that's constantly asking us to go faster, being the person who pauses is a radical act of intention.

The Social Proof & Real World Ripple

I once spoke with a 3rd-grade teacher who told me she dreaded the moment the last bell rang. Not because she didn't love her students (she adores them), but because dismissal time always felt chaotic. Everyone was buzzing with end-of-day energy, questions flying, backpacks half-zipped, kids trying to tell her ten different things at once while she was also answering emails and tidying up. By the time the classroom was empty, she was fried.

So we tried one small move; a 60-second pause. Before dismissal, she would take one full minute. No phone, no grading, no multitasking. Just stillness, a breath, a reset.

The first time felt awkward, like her body didn't know what to do without a task. But by the third week, something had shifted. She didn't snap as often at the end of the day. The classroom felt calmer. The students mirrored her energy instead of escalating it, and she told me: "That pause, it gave me back my patience. It gave me back me."

One breath. One moment. That's the power of the pause.

One of my all-time favorite books when it comes to life, energy, and how we treat each other is *"How Full Is Your Bucket?"* by Tom Rath and Donald Clifton. It's built around a beautifully simple metaphor; each of us has an invisible bucket, and every interaction either fills it or drains it.

Now here's where it gets interesting (and slightly alarming). Research from Gallup shows it can take **five to ten positive interactions** to undo just *one* negative one. That's a lot of smiles, breaths, and "thank you's" just to break even.

And here's the kicker, when we forget to pause, when we snap, criticize, or unload without thinking, we're not just dipping into someone else's bucket, we are draining our own, too. Because giving from an empty bucket?

That's not generosity, it's burnout in disguise. You can't bring good energy into any space if you've got nothing left to give.

Remember back in the *"Bring the Vibe"* section when we talked about protecting your energy? This is a fundamental part of it. There are even whole frameworks around this idea of emotional buckets and energy management and their book nails it in such a simple, memorable way.

So let's bring it down to something real.

Imagine you walk into the kitchen and say to your family, "Let's all just take a breath before we dive into the chaos." Or maybe you send a random "thinking of you" text, or choose not to respond with sarcasm even when it's tempting. What are you really doing? You're tossing a ladleful of good vibes into someone's bucket. You're shifting the tone and quite possibly, their whole day and yours.

> *One pause.*
> *One choice.*
> *One full(er) bucket.*

In a world that's constantly dipping and draining, that kind of Micro-Move isn't just kind, it's radical.

Shed the Funk: Taking the Pause One Step Further

Back on page one, we defined shedding the funk as:

> *"The intentional act of letting go of what's weighing you down;*
> *physically, mentally, emotionally, or energetically.*
> *It's that moment you say: 'Not today, Funk.'"*

As powerful as the pause can be, there are moments when you realize you have skipped the pause completely. You didn't breathe. You didn't reset. You snapped, you spiraled and you let the funk win.

This is where that definition came from. Let me take you back to one of those moments when I didn't just lose the pause, I found the funk instead.

Years ago, I was traveling constantly. I was in a different city every week living out of a suitcase, bouncing from gate to gate, and surviving on hotel coffee and granola bars. One particular morning, I overslept for an early flight. There was no time for breakfast, no time for caffeine, and definitely no time for a deep breath.
Cue: Hangry.

If you have never heard the term, hangry is that delightful combo of hungry and angry, the irritability and short fuse that shows up when your body is running on empty and your patience goes with it. It's science, not just sass. When your blood sugar dips, your brain's ability to regulate emotion takes a hit. You are more likely to snap, stew, or spiral over things that normally wouldn't faze you.

So there I was, hangry, stressed, running late, and spiraling. I reached the TSA with my heart pounding and my stomach louder than the airport announcements. The agent looked at me with that classic airport tone – flat, emotionless, completely unbothered. She said, "ID and boarding pass, please."

And then it happened.

I was already holding back my frustration, annoyed by her complete lack of empathy, trying to keep it together. I was tired, tense and hangry; I reached into my bag and grabbed my wallet, and in one clumsy, hurried motion, it slipped from my hands and it flew open mid-air. Suddenly, coins were everywhere. Scattering, clanging and rolling across the floor like tiny reminders that I had officially lost control of everything; my stuff, my patience, my composure.

It felt like a hundred coins, maybe more. But what it really felt like was defeat. I stood there in silence, watching the mess spread, realizing this wasn't about money or change, it was about me. Something had cracked open and it wasn't just the coin purse.

That was it. The breaking point. The primal scream moment. The straw that broke my composure. I dropped to my knees and started crying, right there in the TSA line. But what happened next changed everything.

A little old man, someone I didn't know and have never seen again, came up behind me and started picking up my change. And no, he wasn't stealing it; he was saving me.

He said, "Honey" (and let me be clear, that's the only time anyone is ever allowed to call me that) "we can't afford for you to get on that plane and infect 150+ people with whatever this is. Your attitude is contagious. Join me in shedding the funk."

And then he started shaking. Like, literally. His hands, his legs, his whole body. This man could barely stand, and yet, here he was, doing the silliest thing to reset my energy. At first, I thought he was nuts. But then, I joined him.

There I was shaking my hands, wiggling my legs, basically doing the hokey pokey in the middle of airport security. Somehow, in the middle of all that ridiculous movement, something shifted. The TSA agents started laughing; I started laughing. Even the guy behind me, who looked like he hadn't smiled since 1998, cracked up. It worked; the funk broke. The tension lifted, and just like that, we were all human again.

That little moment taught me something incredible that I have carried with me ever since; sometimes, the pause isn't just about breathing, it's about shedding the funk. Physically; energetically; emotionally. When the stress builds or my energy feels off, I shed my funk.

I share this with everyone - on stages, in workshops, during one-on-one conversations. It's kind of become my thing. Because movement shifts mindset. Sometimes, the quickest way to reset your brain is through your body.

It's become a part of my daily rhythm. I shake out my hands, bounce my legs, roll my shoulders; most times I look absolutely ridiculous, but every time, I reset.

If you're going to embrace this too, and truly shed the funk, it starts with this: You've got to let go of how it looks and lean into how it feels.

I remember a time when I signed up for something called "ecstatic dance" at a wellness retreat. Now, I've been shedding my funk for years, so I was actually excited about it. It sounded fun, rhythmic, light.

What I imagined was movement with meaning. What I got was a room of thirty-five strangers and zero rules. No choreography, no leader, just music and the instruction to "move however your body wants." For 45 minutes.

Within seconds, I could see it on everyone's face; panic disguised as politeness. Thirty-five strangers stood still, wide-eyed and self-conscious. Some stood frozen. Some giggled nervously. Some clung to their water bottles like emotional support animals. Some were there with friends. Some solo. Some clearly wondered if they could sneak out unnoticed. You could feel the tension in the air.

Who's watching me? Do I look stupid? What if I'm doing it wrong?

But I was there, ready to move. Not to impress. Not to perform. Just to feel free and UnFunkt™. Because you can't shed the funk if you're still performing for the crowd. The fear of being seen as "too much" or "not enough" keeps so many people stuck. But here's the thing; freedom looks awkward to the people still pretending.

So I danced, and maybe I looked ridiculous, but I felt real. The more I moved, the more others started to loosen, smile, move. Because someone always has to go first; not to be brave but to give permission.

We'll talk more about that quiet fear of being watched and compared later in Micro-Move #5: Dare to Compare - Just Don't. But for now? If you're holding back because of who might be watching, they're probably too busy worrying about themselves to notice you anyway.

So move. Speak. Start.
Shed the funk; then help someone else do the same.

Why does this work? It's not just a silly dance, it's wiring. When you move your body, even in small ways, you trigger a release of endorphins - your brain's natural mood boosters. You also get your blood flowing, which brings more oxygen to your brain and helps shake off the mental fog. That quick reset isn't just a vibe shift, it's a physiological one. You're literally changing your chemistry. So yes, a goofy little shake might look silly but it's also backed by science. That's also why people have 30-second dance parties, yes, there's even a button you can buy for that. Whether you're shedding the funk or dancing it off, the key is it needs to move through you. Resetting your mindset isn't optional, it's essential.

Shedding the funk doesn't have to be one-size-fits-all. For some, it's all about that physical release: shaking it off, dancing in the kitchen, or walking it out. For others, it's pairing movement with something that feels restorative - rolling out a yoga mat, strolling with a friend, or simply sitting with a hot cup of coffee and letting your breath slow down. The method is yours to choose; the goal is the same - to shift your energy, reset your headspace, and give yourself the pause you need to show up better for you and for the people around you.

That's the magic; that's the Micro-Move. It doesn't have to be pretty, it just has to be intentional.

Sometimes we miss the pause; we react and we regret it. We replay the moment thinking, "I should've known better."

When we allow ourselves to pause after the stumble, we invite grace instead of shame. It's the moment you step out of the mental replay and remember that being human means sometimes tripping over your own good intentions. It's choosing not to double down on the damage by beating yourself up, but instead to soften, to listen, and to ask, "What can I carry forward from this?" Because grace doesn't excuse what happened, it transforms it; it takes the sting out of the misstep and turns it into a stepping stone.

Swap out *"I should have known better"* for *"Now I know better."*
Then forgive yourself. Because self-shame? That's just self-sabotage in a costume. Growth isn't about perfection; it's about recognition and redirection.

What makes you an even better human isn't getting it right every time, it's learning how to come back clearer, softer, stronger, and with more intention and heart. That's the real power of the pause; it doesn't just change the moment you're in, it changes the next one you walk into.

REFLECTION

Pause with Purpose

Let's take what you've read and bring it into real life.

1. When was the last time you felt emotionally hijacked? What was the situation? What triggered it? What was your immediate reaction?

_____

_____

_____

2. What could you have changed if you had paused first? Shed the funk? What could you have said or done differently with a few seconds of space?

_____

_____

_____

3. List three Micro-Moves that help you reset. These could be deep breaths, grounding phrases, or even physical gestures.

_____

_____

_____

4. Implement Box Breathing:

Start Small: Begin with a few minutes each day, gradually increasing as comfort with the technique grows.

Consistency is Key: Regular practice enhances the benefits, making it easier to employ the technique during stressful situations.

Use as Needed: Beyond daily practice, box breathing can be a go-to tool in moments of acute stress, providing immediate relief and clarity.

5. Write a grounding sentence you can use this week.
   Example: "I have time to respond, not just react."

_____

_____

_____

Keep this page handy. The more often you return to it, the easier the pause becomes.

CHOOSE YOUR NEXT MOVE

3 PAGE 31 ▶ If you're ready to keep building from here, turn the page to **Micro-Move #3: Words Matter. Choose Wisely.**

But if today you're feeling...

9 PAGE 113 ▶ Like your thoughts are racing faster than your clarity? Head to **Micro-Move #9: Listen to Your Second Brain.**

Or feeling...

6 PAGE 75 ▶ Like you've been running nonstop and ignoring what matters most? **Try Micro-Move #6: Be Intentional by Default.**

UnFunkt™

WORDS MATTER CHOOSE WISELY

Your words can

either spark connection

or start a fire.

Choose the kind you want to spread.

Words Matter. Choose Wisely.

Words carry weight. We talked about this back in Micro-Move #1 and how one simple word like hot, positive, or negative can mean wildly different things depending on who's hearing it. One small word, so many interpretations.

Well now, we are about to dive even deeper, because every sentence you speak is either building connection or creating distance. The best communicators? They are not masters of fancy vocabulary, they are masters of intentionality. They choose their words on purpose, not just out of habit.

Want to see what that looks like in real life?

Here's a simple example of how just a few words can completely change the tone, impact, and energy of what you're saying.

Think about the difference between these two phrases:

"You messed this up."
vs.
"Let's walk through what happened and how we can learn from it."

"I have to give this presentation."
vs.
"I get to share this message."

The first ones create stress or shame; the second ones invite growth and connection.

Start noticing your go-to phrases. Replace one limiting phrase a day with something more empowering. For example, swap "I'm so busy" with "My plate is full, and I'm prioritizing what matters."

Language is a tool and you're the craftsman. Shape your words with intention, and you'll shape the culture around you too.

The Words You Choose Change Everything
Because Everyone Has a Different Lens.

In *The 7 Habits of Highly Effective People*, Stephen Covey reminds us that "we see the world not as it is, but as we are." In other words: we're all walking around with our own paradigm, our own mental map based on our past experiences, values, upbringing, fears, and beliefs.

So what sounds "obvious" or "clear" to one person might be completely misunderstood by someone else. That's why language matters so much. Why tone matters. Why curiosity matters.

Instead of assuming people see the situation the way you do, try asking:

"How are you seeing this?"
"What does this look like from your perspective?"
"What do you need from me RIGHT NOW?"

Let's pause for a second before continuing and understand why I bolded **"Right Now."** How two little words can shift the weight of a whole sentence. For a long time, I started my mornings with intention. I'd write something simple like: Lead with kindness; stay curious; be where your feet are. It felt grounding, like a warm-up for the day. But when I tried to end my day with gratitude, things got heavier.

I'd ask myself: What are you grateful for? And suddenly, I felt pressure to come up with something deep or profound or "worthy." The kind of answer that deserved a gold star and a journaling ribbon. (Spoiler: I was usually too tired for that.)

Then one day, I added two little words "right now" and everything shifted. What am I grateful for, right now? Now, it wasn't a task – it was a moment, it was the giggle from a friend's text, the candle I lit, just because, the way the sky looked like it had been painted just for me.

Those words "right now" reduced the pressure and expanded the truth. Then something wild happened. I started using those two words everywhere. Not just in gratitude but in conversations, in journaling, in setting intentions. Suddenly, my questions got clearer. More honest. More human.

What's one goal I have, right now?
How can I help you, right now?
What do I actually need to do, right now?
What's true for me, right now?

"**Right Now**" doesn't erase the big picture. It just makes it actionable. It turns overwhelm into motion. It makes the moment matter.

And it reminds me every day: Words matter, choose them wisely. Even the small ones; especially the small ones.

You will see these two words "right now" pop up throughout this book, because they are more than grounding tools, they are reminders to stay present, ask even better questions, and choose language that invites connection.

When we learn to pause, to ask, to listen, we stop communicating to be right and start communicating to connect, and most times, when we feel a disconnect, it's not what we are asking, it's how we ask it. The wrong language can shut someone down. The right language? It opens the door.

Let's look at another example. Say your team member, your partner, a friend, or even your child, messes up. You could say: "Why did you do that?" But they'll likely feel cornered, judged, or defensive.

Now try one of these instead:

"What made you decide that?"
"What happened that led to this?"
"What's your plan for next time?"

It's the power of "what" instead of "why." "Why" often feels like an accusation.

"What" feels like curiosity.
The result?
Less tension. More trust. Even better conversations.

You may know Simon Sinek's iconic message: Start With Why. He teaches us that great leaders inspire by leading with purpose by communicating their vision, not just the task. But here's what most people miss: Simon's "why" is about your purpose, not your question structure. In emotionally-charged conversations, "why" doesn't build trust, it builds walls.

So here's the connection

Simon says, start with "why" to lead with purpose and meaning;
I say, start with "what" to build trust and open connection in the moment. Because when people feel emotionally safe and seen, they become more open to your message, even your purpose.

Your Why + Their What = Powerful Connection

Your why = the purpose that fuels your decisions, beliefs, and core values. Their what = the bridge that opens trust and invites conversation. Use both.

Start with clarity in your intention and choose words that don't just deliver your point but words that create a space where people feel safe to respond. That's how you build trust, conversation, and connection, one word at a time.

The Science 🗣 Behind the Move

Science backs what you've probably felt; the way we ask questions directly shapes the emotional safety of the conversation. Dr. Amy Edmondson from Harvard coined the term "psychological safety," showing that people perform better, take more risks, and speak more honestly when they feel safe from blame or judgment. And how do we build that safety? Through language.

Researchers like Dr. Marc Brackett and Dr. Andrew Newberg, a psychologist and author of "Words Can Change Your Brain", have found that positive, specific, and curious language activates calm, logical parts of the brain, while vague or critical phrasing, like "why did you do that?" can trigger defensiveness and shut down trust. In contrast, reframing to "what happened that led to this?" creates openness, reflection, and connection. Your tone, your words, and your framing aren't just about being nice, they're about being effective. Positive words strengthen areas in our frontal lobes and promote cognitive function. They can literally change the brain and build better outcomes, one word at a time.

These studies have consistently shown that positive, empowering language not only enhances team morale but improves performance. When leaders reframe problems into possibilities and criticism into coaching, they reduce anxiety and increase engagement.

The bottom line? How we speak doesn't just shape culture, it literally shapes brains.

The Social Proof & Real World Ripple

I remember not too long ago, I was facilitating a workshop in which we were discussing this exact topic; how the words we use shape how we show up and how we see each other. I asked the group: "How many people do you impact or interact with regularly?" A man raised his hand and said, "Oh, I've got 23 people under me." And without even thinking, I said, "Yikes. Under you? That must be uncomfortable." Looking back, I probably should have paused. Sometimes my background in Improv comedy just comes out; I am still perfecting my pause. Ha!

The comment did segue into a really meaningful conversation though. He said it casually, like it was just another day at work, and that's where everything stopped for me. Because words matter, especially the ones we don't even think about. Obviously what he meant was that he managed a team of 23 people. But what he said? That they were under him.

Now, maybe he didn't mean it in a superior way. Maybe it was just a habit. But when someone hears those words "under me," that can land hard. It can sound like a power play, like a reminder of rank, like, you're below me.

It's the same reason I coach organizations not to use the word staff or employee. Those words can feel cold and disconnected. In reality, you are all a team, and when you make the shift to calling someone a team member, something changes. The dynamic softens. The sense of belonging grows. People stop feeling like cogs in a machine and start feeling like contributors to a shared mission.

That is the lesson within the lesson; one small phrase can carry way more meaning than we intended. The words we choose say a lot about what we believe. Sometimes, those tiny words carry the biggest weight. They can reveal how we view others. They can make people feel small or worse, invisible. And they can absolutely fracture connection before it even begins.

That's the thing about words and phrases. The same word or phrase can carry completely different meanings depending on who's hearing it and how they're hearing it. We all come from different places with different stories, and different definitions. What sounds clear to one person might feel like a jab to another; that's why clarity matters. That's why checking in matters and that's why the best conversations aren't just about being heard, they're about making sure it lands. So, choose your words wisely.

The Language Shift with "Even Better"

By now, you may have noticed something. I don't say "better." I say "even better."

Here's why.
"Better" can feel like what came before wasn't good enough. Like something was wrong with you, your effort, or your story. But "even better?" That leaves room for growth without judgment. It honors where you've been while opening the door to what's next. It's not a correction. It's an expansion.

So let me tell you an even better story because sometimes the words we choose shape more than the sentence. They shape the story we tell ourselves next.

There's a phrase I often say because it keeps proving itself true:

"The words we use directly impact the results we get."

My husband once asked me what I meant by that, so I gave him a real-world example. I told him I never just say, "Be better at this." Even with good intentions, it can sound condescending, like they are not already doing a good job.

It can trigger defensiveness, even when you're trying to be encouraging. Instead, I add one simple word, "even." As in: "You could be even better." It is subtle, but the shift in energy is huge.

I encouraged him to test it out in the car with our daughter who, for the record, is already really good at math. (Also worth noting, some of my greatest case studies live right under my roof. Sorry, family, it's all fair game.)

My husband looked at her and said, "You know, I believe you can be better at math." Yikes. Cue the attitude.

Our sweet 9-year-old went full defense mode: "What do you mean I can be better? I am good at math!" And she wasn't wrong. The problem was she wasn't hearing encouragement; she was hearing critique.

Then I gently jumped in and said, "Hey sweetie, I believe you can be "even" better at math."

It was like a flipped switch. The energy in the car completely changed. She softened, got curious, and she leaned in. "What do you mean?" she asked.

Now, not that parenting is ever a competition but let's just say that was one point for mommy; all thanks to the power of "even." That's the incredible power of one word.

That's the Micro-Move. This principle shows up in everyday conversations all the time.

I recently spoke with a friend who was frustrated that the people around her weren't stepping up. Whether it was her partner, her kids, or her volunteer group, she kept saying, "You need to be more proactive." In her mind, that meant noticing what needed to be done without being asked, taking ownership of tasks, pitching in without reminders, and anticipating needs before they became problems.

Her intention was to motivate. But the result? Silence. Shrugs. Maybe even a few eye rolls. So we talked about reframing. Instead of calling out what was missing, what if she called attention to what she believed was already there?

I encouraged her to try a new approach by changing her words. So she did. With her partner, instead of saying, "You never help with dinner," she began with, "You're great at pulling a meal together quickly, can you help make tonight's dinner even better by handling the sides?" With her kids, she swapped, "You need to clean up your mess," for, "You've shown me how responsible you can be, how about we make this room look even better together?" With her coworkers, instead of, "You all need to speak up more in meetings," she led with, "I've seen how thoughtful and resourceful you all are. I'd love to hear your ideas on how we could make this project even better moving forward." Just like that, the energy shifted. People leaned in and ideas started flowing. There was less defensiveness and more collaboration. That one micro phrase did something powerful; it created psychological safety.

As I mentioned earlier, psychological safety is a concept first studied by Dr. Amy Edmondson from Harvard; it's the belief that you can speak up, take risks, or share honestly without fear of being punished or humiliated. While the term is often used in workplace settings, it applies just as much at the dinner table, in friend groups, and in everyday relationships. Because when people feel safe, they speak up, and when they feel seen, they step in. How do we build that safety? Through language.

It often starts with small word choices. The right words can create safety, whereas the wrong words create silence. The words we use directly impact the results we get.

REFLECTION

Words Matter. Choose Wisely.

Let's turn awareness into actions, because the words you speak shape the culture around you.

What's one phrase you catch yourself saying that might unintentionally limit, discourage, or shut someone down?
(Think tone, timing, or word choice. Even a good intention can land wrong.)
Now rewrite that phrase.

_____

_____

_____

How can you say it in a way that empowers, includes, or uplifts?
Try a reframe that feels real, not robotic.

_____

_____

_____

Think back to a moment when someone's words lit a fire in you.
What did they say? How did it land?

_____

_____

_____

More importantly, how did it make you feel seen, valued, or motivated?

_____

_____

_____

Practice the "Even Better" shift. Who can you lift this week by using the simple phrase:

"You're doing great, and you know what would make it even better?"

_____

_____

_____

Words Matter.

Write, reflect, and revisit this page whenever your conversations start feeling stale or when you need to reset your impact.

CHOOSE YOUR NEXT MOVE

4 PAGE 45 ▶ If you're ready to keep building from here, turn the page to **Micro-Move #4: Dare to Compare – Just Don't.**

But if today you're feeling...

10 PAGE 125 ▶ Like your words aren't landing the way you want them to? **Go to Micro-Move #10: Own Your Impact.**

Or feeling...

8 PAGE 103 ▶ Like you've forgotten to celebrate how far you've come? **Skip to Micro-Move #8: Celebrate Small Wins.**

UnFunkt™

—— Micro-Move #4 ——

DARE TO COMPARE JUST DON'T

Comparison kills your sparkle,

and you were never meant to dim.

Dare to Compare – Just Don't

We've all done it.
You're scrolling Instagram
flawless vacations, perfectly styled homes, high-achieving kids.

You open LinkedIn
another promotion, big speaking gig, "so-humbled-to-be-honored" award.

You flip through Facebook
third marathon this year, while you're still trying to make it to the gym twice a month.

You're in a meeting
someone nails the perfect idea, tells the story that wins the room, gets instant praise.

You're at school pickup
another parent talks about their child's straight A's.

You visit a friend's home
it's spotless, while your sink is full of dishes.

Just like that, you have built an entire case against yourself without the other person even knowing they were in the competition. That's the trap of comparison, and it's one of the fastest ways to drain your confidence, your energy, and your joy.

Comparison creates distortion. You're comparing their highlight reel to your behind-the-scenes and their "polished post" to your "work in progress." They are on their chapter 20 while you might be on your chapter 4. That's not just unfair, it's unhelpful. Comparison doesn't motivate, it paralyzes; it doesn't challenge, it clouds. Most importantly, it pulls you out of your own lane, where your actual impact is waiting.

The Science 🗣 Behind the Move

Author, Brené Brown, calls comparison "the crush of conformity." It's that moment when we stop seeing ourselves clearly and instead start measuring our worth by someone else's metrics. How we look, what we've achieved, how many likes we've racked up, or whether we're "keeping up."

It's exhausting, and it's dangerous.

A landmark study published in The Journal of Social and Clinical Psychology found a direct correlation between increased time on social media and higher rates of anxiety, depression, and decreased self-esteem. The more we scroll, the more we compare. The more we compare, the worse we feel, especially when we engage in upward comparison, perceiving others as having "more."

Why? Because we tend to compare our messy middle to someone else's polished peak, and in that gap, shame loves to settle. The good news? There is an antidote.

Dr. Kristin Neff, a pioneer in the field of self-compassion, found that people who focus inward with kindness and curiosity, instead of outward with comparison, are significantly more resilient. They are better equipped to navigate challenges, setbacks, and those "not enough" moments that creep in when we measure ourselves against someone else's journey.

Neff's research shows that self-compassion isn't just feel-good fluff, it's a performance strategy. People who treat themselves with grace don't just feel better, they perform better, recover faster, and stay in the game longer. Translation? Looking left and right won't help you move forward. But looking inward with curiosity instead of criticism just might.

The other thing to note is that it's never oranges to oranges. We compare as if we're all working from the same starting line, but we're not. We don't know what people have sacrificed, suffered, or struggled through to get to their "highlight moment." Yet, we scroll and assume. We measure our middle against their milestones.

But success isn't a one-size-fits-all story.

Popcorn is prepared in the same pot, in the same heat, in the same oil, and yet the kernels do NOT all pop at the same time. Don't compare yourself to others. Your turn to POP will come!

I once read about a mother and daughter walking the marina in Cape Cod, admiring the yachts. They kept saying things like, "Wow, it must be nice to be that rich." But then they paused in front of one yacht that stood out. It belonged to Jan Koum, the co-founder of WhatsApp. Yes, the same man who went on to sell his company to Facebook for a staggering $19 billion. Sounds like a dream, right?

But what they didn't see was the full story. Koum immigrated from Ukraine with his mother, lived in a small apartment, and relied on food stamps. He lost his mother to cancer. He applied for a job at Facebook and was rejected. Then after all of that, he built WhatsApp, eventually selling it to the very company that once told him "no."

So yes, he has the yacht now. But would you really want to trade places if it meant living through every single one of those battles? The grief? The poverty? The rejection? Most of us wouldn't. And it's not just billionaires; this theme shows up in everyday success stories, too.

In one of my favorite episodes of my daughter-father podcast "What's Your Story? with Jaime & Stan", we sat down with the effortlessly fabulous Lauren Hitchen, Principal CEO at The Jetset Travel Group. Her Instagram feed is pure travel glamor. Think five-star resorts, yacht days, and dream destinations. You see it and think: "Must be nice."

But here's what you don't see and what you wouldn't guess from her picture-perfect grid. Her parents moved to Florida from Berwick-upon-Tweed, which is a small little town, nestled between England and Scotland. Lauren's childhood bedroom wasn't in some beachfront villa. It was inside an assisted living facility.

They moved to start a new life and that new life came with 16 rooms, only one of which was available for Lauren some of the time. At 16 years old, though she didn't meet the age requirement, she was definitely part of the crew. Her room? Rented out to new residents when space was tight. "Sorry, darling," her mum would say, "Your room was so nice, I sold it." So Lauren moved from room to room, and when every last one was taken, she lived in a hotel.

When she went to college, she was packed into a van with the residents from the assisted living facility, all cheering her on for her big day at the local community college. The facility's calendar literally said, "Lauren goes to college," and it was a field trip for the whole community. If Netflix is looking for its next quirky hit, Lauren's life is ready for a green light. But behind the sitcom-level moments was something deeper.

There were no shortcuts. No silver spoon. As an immigrant without a social security number, Lauren couldn't even get a job, let alone a credit card or a mortgage. But what she could do was hustle. She helped in the facility when someone didn't show up. She washed dishes. She did what had to be done. And now? Lauren curates luxury travel for clients jetting off to the most stunning corners of the globe. Five-star everything. Custom itineraries. Champagne on arrival.

She didn't inherit the dream, she built it. Room by room, hustle by hustle. With grit, vision, and the kind of work ethic you don't post about but feel in your bones. As she said in the episode (with that signature British understatement): "It didn't happen overnight. I put in the work. And we all have the same number of hours in the day."

So no, it's never apples to apples. Or even oranges to oranges. It's oranges to thunderstorms. Success to sleepless nights. Applause to the kind of behind-the-scenes hustle you'll never see in an Instagram post.

So, stop measuring your life against someone else's most photogenic moment. Stay focused on the story you are actually writing. The one that's still unfolding. The one that's uniquely yours.

The Social Proof & Real World Ripple

The Night I Almost Let Comparison Win:

After graduating college, I landed what I thought was my dream job, working for Royal Caribbean Cruise Lines as an onboard team member. And honestly, it was a dream. I got paid to travel the world, host karaoke nights, and make people laugh for a living. My office view was the open sea. My coworkers were from every corner of the globe. My daily uniform? A name badge, a big smile, and the energy to light up a crowd. Oh and on embarkation days? Pantyhose, polyester skirts, heels, and a scarf. Ugh. Nothing says "Welcome Aboard" quite like sweating through synthetic fabrics in 98% humidity while trying to keep your scarf from strangling you in the wind!

Working on a cruise ship was an incredible experience. It was my real-world MBA, minus the textbooks, with a lot more costumes and buffets. I learned how to work with people from every culture, think on my feet when plans went sideways, and keep smiling even when the coffee machine broke right before a 6 a.m. tour. It taught me adaptability, resilience, and the art of connecting with just about anyone, all while navigating a floating city in the middle of the ocean.

It taught me what it really means to show up, to build a work ethic rooted in consistency, teamwork, and pride, and to bring my best, every day, because people were counting on me to make their trip unforgettable; that kind of responsibility shapes you in the best way.

I also met people from all over the world with different languages, different customs, and different ways of thinking. I learned to connect across cultures, adapt quickly, and build bridges with humor, patience, and respect. It wasn't just a job; it was an experience that sharpened my emotional intelligence, tested my resilience, and gave me a whole new appreciation for teamwork and hustle. It changed how I show up in life and in business, because when you're part of a team that's responsible for creating joy on the high seas, you learn that every moment matters and every role counts.

In my role, I started out as general cruise staff – you know, the one handing out ping pong paddles and trying to herd latecomers into trivia. But thanks to my advanced skills in small talk, hype, and getting strangers to dance like no one's watching, I was promoted to Social Host. That meant I got to do a little bit of everything - game shows, dance parties, bingo, theme nights, karaoke, and yes... performing. Basically, I was a walking energy drink.

One of our most beloved performances was the final-night comedy sketch called "If I Were Not Upon the Sea." It was legendary. A full cast of characters and complete chaos. The comedic cherry on top of the week. The skit had a series of repeating characters with punchlines, silly props, and physical comedy, and each had their own rhyming couplet.

Imagine each member of the entertainment team stepping forward to announce what they would be if they weren't working at sea and then acting it out in full costume and character. The cruise director might say: "If I were not upon the sea, a ballerina, me" and then twirl across the stage in a tutu three sizes too small. Or the head of activities declaring: "If I were not upon the sea, a firefighter, me" only to get blasted with a water gun mid-routine. It was loud, it was silly, and it was pure gold.

I'll never forget the first time I was asked to perform the final-night comedy bit. As social host, it was my turn to join and it was in the role of lighthouse keeper. The lighthouse keeper was always a crowd favorite, and maybe a little scandalous depending on how it was performed. Other hosts had done it before me, and they were hilarious. Crowd favorites; standing ovations. So naturally, the pressure started bubbling.

> *"I hope I'm as funny."*
> *"What if they liked the last girl more?"*
> *"What if I blow it?"*

I was spiraling before I even got to the mic. Then I paused. I remembered something that's now a core part of what I teach. You don't need to be someone else's version of great. You just need to be fully you.

So I showed up and I brought my version of the role. I played, I connected, and I let the fun be the focus, not the fear. And guess what? The audience laughed. They leaned in and they clapped like crazy. Not because I outperformed anyone else but because I showed up as me.

Now, full transparency: As the lighthouse keeper I had on a giant yellow raincoat and underneath it? A bathing suit. When it was time for my part, I had to sing:

> *"If I were not upon the sea, there's something else I'd rather be.*
> *If I were not upon the sea, a lighthouse keeper, me!*
> *Happy all day long and this would be my song...*

"With a quick flash here and a quick flash there," at which point I would open the coat even bigger and flash even more, "turning round and round." Then we all repeated our parts in unison and, somehow, every single one managed to interact with the person next to them in the most ridiculous, and arguably inappropriate, way possible.

And I was paired with the "taxi driver," whose go-to move was a dramatic honk-the-horn gesture that, unfortunately for me, involved my personal space. Thankfully, there is no known footage of that wildly ridiculous, definitely not HR-approved performance floating around the internet. (Let's keep it that way.)

The moral of the story? We're all performing in some way. On stages, in meetings, on social media, at work events, and on first dates. We compare ourselves, wondering if we're smart enough, funny enough, successful enough. But comparison will always steal your spotlight. Authenticity is what makes you shine.

So, what's the Micro-Move here?

DO YOU. BY YOU. FOR YOU.

No one does it better. Move from envy to inspiration. From comparison to curiosity. Next time you catch yourself comparing, try this instead:

Ask, "What's this moment trying to show me?" Then say, "Good for them and I'm growing too."

Also, it's really important to remember, you are not behind, you are just on your own timeline. And your timeline is exactly where you are supposed to be. Sometimes that mindset shift isn't so easy and we can get stuck in a comparison spiral. Here's a Micro-Move that starts before you even leave the house, high five your reflection.

Yes, seriously.

This concept comes from Mel Robbins, bestselling author of The High 5 Habit. She created this practice during a time when she was feeling low, lost, and overwhelmed. Like so many of us, she found that when she looked in the mirror, her first instinct was to critique herself. So instead, she tried something radical and ridiculously simple; she gave herself a high five. Why? Because the brain already associates a high five with celebration, support, and encouragement. You don't need to say anything. Just the gesture alone triggers a positive emotional and neurological response.

When you high five your reflection, you're telling your brain: "I've got you. You're worth showing up for. You're on your way." And sometimes, that's all it takes to start the day with self-compassion instead of self-comparison.

Here's something else that shifted my perspective; I once heard someone say, "When someone's sharing their goodness, it's not bragging. It's sharing." That stuck with me. Because sometimes we confuse someone's celebration with self-centeredness. But most of the time, people aren't trying to one-up you. They are just proud; they are excited. They are processing, and they deserve that moment.

So let them share. Let them shine. Just don't compare and let their success impact your path to happiness.

Remember, someone else's spotlight doesn't cancel out your own. Just because they're shining doesn't mean you're not. There's room for all of us to glow; just don't let their light dim yours. Their celebration doesn't diminish yours. You don't lose anything by letting someone feel good about their win. In fact, it's the opposite – you gain a moment of grace, growth, and groundedness. Because when you let others shine without shrinking yourself, you're not just skipping comparison, you're leading by example.

REFLECTION

Dare to Compare – Just Don't

Let's flip the lens, because the only path that matters is yours..

1. What's one area of your life where comparison shows up most often?
   (Social media? Career? Parenting? Your relationship? Your pace?)

_____

_____

_____

2. How does that comparison actually make you feel?
   Is it pushing you forward or quietly draining your joy?

_____

_____

_____

3. List three things you're genuinely proud of in your own journey right now.
   (Big or small; progress is personal.)

1. _____

2. _____

3. _____

4. When was the last time someone reflected something good back to you, something they admired, or appreciated? What did they say? How did you take it?

_____

_____

_____

5. Try this mantra this week:

"I don't need to match their pace. I just need to honor my own path."

Say it. Write it. Live it. Especially when the scroll starts to whisper.

_____

_____

_____

CHOOSE YOUR NEXT MOVE

5 PAGE 59 ▶ If you're ready to keep building from here, turn the page to **Micro-Move #5: Fuel Others with Appreciation.**

But if today you're feeling...

10 PAGE 125 ▶ Caught in self-doubt or imposter syndrome? Try **Micro-Move #10: Own Your Impact.**

Or feeling...

6 PAGE 75 ▶ Ready to shift from inner spiral to outward gratitude? Flip ahead to **Micro-Move #6: Be Intentional by Default.**

UnFunkt™

FUEL OTHERS WITH APPRECIATION

Gratitude is free, portable,

and instantly renewable.

Hand it out like candy.

Fuel Others with Appreciation

We all want to feel seen, valued, and acknowledged, not just for the big wins, but for the everyday moments when we show up and give our best. Appreciation is more than a polite "thank you." It's fuel. The kind that powers motivation, deepens connection, and inspires people to keep going.

Let's talk about standing ovations. Remember when those were a thing? I mean a full-on, crowd-to-their-feet, clapping-until-their-palms-hurt moment of genuine, unfiltered celebration? From elementary school stages to Broadway shows, a standing ovation used to be how we said: "You gave it your all and we saw you." It was an invitation for the performers to "soak it in." A way of saying, "That mattered; you matter."

But lately, I feel like it happens less and less. I realized it during one of my daughter's recent school performances. After the music stopped and the kids took their bow, I stood, I clapped, and I cheered like the proud mom I am. But then I looked around and noticed something. I was the only one of a few people standing, and not just at that performance, but at most assemblies, recitals, and ceremonies I'd been to recently, and it made me wonder...

When did we stop standing for people? Not just literally, but figuratively, too?

When did it become easier to nod politely or scroll past the announcement than to actually "celebrate" someone's effort? When did our default become quiet acknowledgment instead of loud appreciation? Appreciation isn't something extra; it's essential.

When someone pours themselves into something, whether it's a school play, a work project, a presentation, or just showing up when it was hard, the most powerful gift we can give them is to let them know they were seen. Because appreciation doesn't just recognize the effort, it amplifies it. It makes people want to give more, to lead more, to show up more.

Here's the best part – appreciation costs nothing, but it pays off in energy, connection, motivation, and loyalty. So, whether you're clapping in an auditorium or complimenting a coworker, don't underestimate the power of standing.

Stand for the effort.
Stand for courage.
Stand for them showing up.

And if you're wondering whether it's too much? It probably means it's just enough.

The Science Behind the Move

Appreciation isn't fluffy, it's foundational.

According to a Gallup study, employees who receive regular recognition are:

- **4 times more likely to be engaged at work.**
- **5 times more likely to feel connected to company culture.**
- **And 73% less likely to feel burned out.**

And that's not just in the office. In classrooms, in sports teams, and in families, when people feel seen and appreciated, performance goes up and resilience builds. Here's the kicker; nearly 65% of people say they haven't received a single word of appreciation in the last year. Let that sink in.

That means we're surrounded by people, kids, colleagues, cashiers doing their best, giving their energy, holding it all together and not feeling like it matters.

We can do better. We must do better.

The Real Power of Appreciation:
Who You Are > What You Do.

Let's break down two phrases:

"I appreciate that you helped me with the report."

"I appreciate you."

Both are positive. Both express gratitude. But only one of them gets to the core of someone's value. Because appreciating someone for what they do is situational; it's conditional. It's nice, but it often feels like a transaction. Appreciating someone for who they are? That's lasting. That's identity-level.

That's relational.
It says you matter, not just because of what you've done, but because of who you are when you walk into the room. Yet, we so often default to the checklist kind of appreciation.

You know the kind:

A quick "thanks!" in an email or text.

A passing "good job!" in a hallway.

Maybe even a generic shout-out in a meeting slide.

It counts, sure. But does it really make someone feel appreciated? Like, deep down, seen-for-who-you-are, kind of appreciation.

Now compare that to a handwritten thank-you note. Not an email. A real, pen-to-paper, hand-cramping-from-writing, kind of note. When was the last time you sent one? Better yet, when was the last time you received one? Funny how that works. Every time I send one, I get a thank you for the thank you! That's how rare it is. But also how deeply it lands.

And I've seen that impact play out firsthand. I was recently teaching a leadership class and, as I always do, I introduced the concept of appreciation through handwritten thank-you notes. Every single time I bring it up, I get the same mixed reaction, some people roll their eyes, some give me the polite "yeah, sure" smile, and a few look like they're silently thinking, there is no way I'm doing that. And that's fine because I'll keep telling people how powerful a handwritten thank-you note is until the day I die.

A few weeks after that session, one of the most macho guys in the group came up to me and asked if I had a minute. Now, I don't usually lean into stereotypes, but this was not someone who seemed like the sentimental type. He told me that after the class, he thought: What the heck, I'll write a note.

So he did. He wrote a thank-you note to the head plumber in his organization's facilities team; he left it on the guy's workspace. Later that week, the plumber stopped by his office, holding the note, on the verge of tears. He said: "In my 25 years of working here, I have never once received a thank-you note. Actually, I've never in my life received one that was handwritten."

The seemingly "macho guy" admitted it brought him to tears too. They stood there, two grown men, having a real, human moment. He told me: "From that day forward, I've never underestimated the power of saying thank you." Side note, I've never, ever, met someone who didn't light up after receiving a genuine, handwritten thank-you card. (Okay, maybe if you mail it to their home address without having a reason to know it, it might feel a little stalker-ish, but even then, they would probably still keep it!)

The key is authenticity; not the pre-printed kind with stock phrases and company logos but the kind in which your words are specific, heartfelt, and personal. But it goes even deeper than that, because how we show appreciation matters just as much as what we say.

You've no doubt heard of the Golden Rule: Treat others how you want to be treated.

Here is an example of the Golden Rule in action: Let's say, as a thank you for reading this book, I had a gift shipped to your house. A big, greasy, golden bucket of french fries. Sounds amazing, right?

Well, maybe. I mean, I love french fries. I love them so much my best friend Uber Eats them to my house every year on my birthday. But what if you don't love them? What if you don't eat fried food? What if you are a waffle fry purist?

Though a sweet idea and well-intentioned, that gift was all about how I like to be appreciated, not how you do. So, let's upgrade the Golden Rule because we can do even better. It's not just that you appreciate someone; it's how you show it that makes the difference.

Knowing what that small move is for that person in your world is where real connection lives. It's the difference between the Golden Rule and the Platinum Rule (treat others the way they want to be treated).

One is thoughtful; the other is transformational. Appreciation isn't one-size-fits-all. It's not about doing what would make you feel seen, it's about taking the time to learn what makes someone else feel seen.

The Platinum Rule shows up in all kinds of little ways...

One of my favorite ways to bring the Platinum Rule to life in my workshops is through food, which, if you've been paying attention, you've probably noticed I bring up a lot. What can I say? Snacks are my love language! They are also a shortcut to connection.

Before I ever walk into a classroom or a workshop, I ask questions to understand with whom I'm working, not just their titles or roles, but the humans behind the name tags. One of my all-time favorite questions? "What's your favorite snack?" Now, that might sound small, but let me tell you – it's not. Because once I know their favorite snack, guess what shows up at their table? That exact snack!

Sometimes it's a bag of Flamin' Hot Cheetos.
Sometimes it's a very specific brand of beef jerky I have to hunt down across three counties, or Trader Joe's okra snacks – always a wildcard.

I once bought a Red Lobster gift card because someone listed crab legs as their favorite snack and I wasn't about to stink up the training room with shellfish. Then there was the time I Insta-Carted ice cream so it'd arrive just in time and not melt before the session. I once tracked down a wildly obscure flavor of Pop-Tarts because, apparently, Frosted Cherry is a personality trait. When they walk in and see their snack waiting for them their whole face changes. Why? Because knowing what lights people up, their quirks, their favorites, their go-to snacks, matters. It's not just a treat. It's about feeling seen, considered, cared for. Not because they did anything special but simply because they were known.

That's appreciation in action. That's the Platinum Rule. Not "Here's what I think you'll like," but: "Here's what you told me matters and I listened."
It's not about the snack, it's about communicating the message "you matter."
If I treated everyone the way I like to be treated, they would be getting french fries. And while I stand by french fries, real appreciation means thinking beyond ourselves.

The same goes for how we show appreciation at work or in our personal relationships. Some people love public praise, others want a handwritten note, others feel seen when you take something off their plate and others light up when you simply remember how they take their coffee, or that maybe they don't drink coffee at all.

Appreciation isn't about grand gestures; it's about thoughtful ones. It's not about what you would want, it's about knowing who they are and showing them that they matter. That's when appreciation turns into fuel. Not just a feel-good moment, but a spark that builds trust, belonging, and real connection.

The real power of appreciation isn't based on what someone does; it's grounded in who they are.

The Platinum Rule is what changes the game. It asks:

- **"How do you feel seen?"**
- **"What makes you feel appreciated for just being you?"**
- **"When do you feel most valued, not for what you did, but for who you are?"**

When we stop assuming and start asking, we shift appreciation from performance to presence. At the end of the day, people don't just want to be valued for what they do. They want to be seen for who they are. It's not always about grand gestures either. Sometimes, it starts with something small, something personal, something as simple as a name.

Let's talk about one of the simplest, most powerful forms of appreciation – using someone's name.

Not a nickname you made up.
Not "Hey you."
Not "Champ," "Chief," or "Hun."
Their actual name.

It might seem small, but remembering someone's name, and pronouncing it correctly, is one of the quickest ways to make someone feel seen. When you say their name, what you're really saying is: "I noticed you; I remembered you; you matter enough to me that I didn't just let you blend in."

I really like to use people's names. There is just something really powerful about it. So, when I'm given a list of attendees ahead of time, I study it. Not just the names, but the people behind them. I learn the pronunciations, I look for patterns, and I try to get a sense of who's in the room before I ever step into it. That way, when we do meet, I'm not meeting a crowd, I'm meeting individuals.

If it's a live event with a larger audience, I do my best to walk the room beforehand and meet as many people as I can because it helps me personalize the message, connect more genuinely, and remind everyone that they are not just part of a crowd – they matter.

Do I always get it right? Of course not. But do I try? Every time. Because I don't just want to show up and speak at people, I want to connect with them. Names aren't just labels, they're connection points. And when you fuel others with appreciation, names aren't optional, they're essential.

One of the most meaningful activities I do in my workshops is an activity called "The Conversation Stack." I put my spin on an old Dale Carnegie memory hack, but with a modern, connection-first twist. We start by learning a simple, powerful tool to help teams genuinely connect, not just network. It's especially helpful for those awkward moments when small talk feels like a chore. (If I hear one more person open with, "So, what do you do?" I might actually keel over. I'm on a mission to upgrade the world's conversations. Surprised? Didn't think so!)

The first step in the conversation stack? Learning someone's name and remembering it. How often does someone introduce themselves and you forget their name before they've even finished saying it?

I teach a quick trick to lock it in and then we build from there. By the end, we're not just talking about it, we're up and practicing it. My favorite part? When I pause and ask: "Does anyone have a story behind their name? Maybe why it was it given to you?" That's when the magic happens.

Even in rooms where people have worked together for years, brand-new stories emerge. You'll hear someone say: "I've known you for 20 years and never knew that!" Suddenly, that name you've heard 100 times carries whole new weight.

"I was named after my grandmother who survived the war."

"I was given a name that means 'hope' in my family's language."

"My name? It was chosen because it was the only thing my parents agreed on."

And then another person pipes up,
"I'm 52 and have no idea where my name came from!"

Regardless of their answers, every time, the room gets quiet. Not because it's sad but because it's sacred. It's a reminder that behind every name tag is a human; with a story, with a history, and with heart.

Taking a moment to ask, learn, and remember? It may seem like a little thing, but it's one of the best ways to show someone you truly see them. Because appreciation isn't always loud; sometimes, it's as simple as saying someone's name, pronouncing it correctly, and truly meaning it.

The Social Proof & Real World Ripple

The Standing Ovation That Stuck

You already heard how it hit me. Standing solo at my daughter's school performance, clapping like a proud mom while almost everyone else sat politely. But this impact? It hit the workplace.

I was delivering a keynote at a recognition ceremony for one of my clients. It was a beautiful event – awards, speeches, spotlight moments. But something was missing. Appreciation was happening but not being "felt." As each person went up to accept their award, no one stood. There were no cheers, just polite claps and camera flashes. You could feel how much it meant to the award recipients, but you could also feel how quietly it passed.

So I stood up.

First for one. Then another. Slowly, other people started standing too, one by one. It wasn't loud or flashy, but by the end, every single honoree was receiving a room on their feet. Did I guilt them into it? Maybe a little. Did it take up more time? Yes. But the risk is worth the reward. It was something deeper, a reminder that appreciation is contagious.

It reminded me of a viral video I once saw. It was a social experiment in which a group of actors were put in a waiting room and instructed to stand every time a bell rang. At first, it seemed odd but quickly, a fascinating thing happened. As new people entered the room, they watched the others and slowly, without knowing why, they also stood when they heard the bell. Why?

Because people follow behavior, especially visible behavior. So, what does that teach us? That standing up for celebration, for recognition, for people, isn't just a moment; it's a movement. And sometimes, all it takes is one person going first. Be that person, unapologetically.

The Micro-Move:
See It. Say It. Stand for It.

Here's your challenge: Start today – practice the "Three S's of Appreciation":

1. "See it":
Notice when someone gives effort. Whether it's your barista remembering your order or your teammate staying late to help.

_____

_____

2. "Say it":
Don't just think it, say it. Out loud. Write a sticky note. Make a call. Send a text. Speak the gratitude you're holding inside.

_____

_____

3. "Stand for it":
When someone shines, don't be afraid to stand, literally or figuratively. Celebrate them in a meeting. Clap in public. Cheer loudly. Be the spark that others follow.

_____

_____

What we appreciate, we amplify. And that impact can be bigger than we'll ever know.

Why It Matters More Than You Think

Think a compliment won't make a difference? Think again.

Research highlighted in the *Harvard Business Review* reveals something we often underestimate – just how much a few kind words can impact someone.

Researchers found that people regularly overestimate how awkward it will be to give a compliment, and underestimate how good it will make the other person feel. That means we're sitting on a superpower and not using it. The takeaway? If you're hesitating to say: "I appreciated the way you handled that conversation," or "Dinner was delicious," or "Thanks for listening when I needed to vent," odds are it will matter way more to the other person than you realize. The same study found that recipients consistently reported feeling flattered, happy, and valued, and often far more than the giver expected.

So, here's your Micro-Move. Don't hoard the good thoughts. If you admire someone's attitude, effort, or even their shoes, say it. What feels small to you might be the bright spot in someone else's day.

REFLECTION

Fuel Others with Appreciation

Let's put this into action:

1. Who's one person you deeply appreciate but haven't told lately?
   How can you show them you see who they are, not just what they do?

   _____

   _____

   _____

2. What's one small, specific detail you've learned about someone?
   Like their favorite snack, drink, or hobby that you could reflect back
   to them this week as a form of appreciation?

   _____

   _____

   _____

3. When was the last time you felt genuinely appreciated? What made it
   meaningful and did it have anything to do with someone honoring your
   preferences or personality?

   _____

   _____

   _____

4. What's the story behind your name and how would it feel if someone took the time to ask or remember it? Now flip it. Whose name do you want to learn (or say correctly) this week?

_____

_____

_____

5. This week, choose one person a day and fuel them with appreciation that fits them. Not how you like to receive it, but how they do.

_____

_____

_____

CHOOSE YOUR NEXT MOVE

6 PAGE 75 ▶ If you're ready to keep building from here, turn the page to **Micro-Move #6: Be Intentional by Default.**

But if today you're feeling...

2 PAGE 12 ▶ Like your days are on autopilot? Turn back to **Micro-Move #2: Pause with Purpose.**

Or feeling...

7 PAGE 85 ▶ Like you've been holding it all in? Flip to **Micro-Move #7: Normalize Asking for Help.**

UnFunkt™

BE INTENTIONAL BY DEFAULT

Don't let your day drive you.
Grab the wheel and point it
where you actually want to go.

Be Intentional by Default

Presence isn't performative, it's about being vulnerable, and that's why most people avoid it. Because true presence requires intention; you have to choose to show up, not just be in the room.

I remember a time when I was sitting in a café, just me, a warm mug, and a few precious minutes to be still. I looked around and noticed something. Every single person, at every single table, was on their phone. Scrolling. Tapping. Zoning out.

Even people sitting across from each other weren't with each other. They were in their own little digital worlds, heads down, eyes glazed. I get it; we've all been there. It's easy. It's automatic. It's addicting. A simple glance turns into a scroll spiral. A second becomes ten minutes. We disconnect without even noticing we're doing it. But that day, for whatever reason, I didn't grab my phone. I sat there. Just me and my thoughts.

At first, I felt present. Then I felt... exposed.

It was like I had forgotten my armor. Like I was doing something wrong by simply being. My brain got loud. Thoughts I hadn't had space for started to flood in.

Worries, ideas, feelings I hadn't wanted to feel. But then, something else arrived.

Stillness made space, and in that space, I started to see and feel the world again. The warmth of the mug in my hands, the breath in my chest, and the quiet but powerful reminder that, despite the noise of the world, I was still here.

That moment reminded me of something to which I keep coming back to, presence is not a punishment, it's a gift we've forgotten how to hold. When we pair presence with intention, that's when everything begins to shift.

Because being intentionally present isn't just about silence or stillness. It's about choosing to be where you are right now. To notice, to listen, to lead with the energy for which the moment actually calls.

It's the kind of presence that strengthens connection, invites authenticity, and transforms the way we show up for our lives and for each other. Presence changes your awareness; intention changes your impact.

When you practice both, even in a small moment, even over coffee, it doesn't just change the moment – it changes you.

Presence, energy, awareness, and intention don't exist in isolation. They swirl together, they influence each other, and they all start with one small moment of noticing. Put down the phone. Tune into the room. Choose your frequency.

That's how we shift from autopilot to awareness and from just doing things to doing them with purpose. Because when we become more intentional in how we speak, lead, listen, move, and connect, we stop going through the motions and start making a real impact.

When I talk about being intentional, I don't mean planning every detail of your day or mapping out your life like a five-year strategy plan. I mean choosing how you want to show up before the world chooses for you.

Because without that pause, without that choice, we default to whatever energy we are carrying from the last thing. The stress from the email, the mood from the group text, the noise of the news, and suddenly, we are being reactive rather than proactive.

The Science 🗣 Behind the Move

Studies from Florida State University show that when we make too many unplanned, reactive decisions throughout the day, we reduce our brain's ability to focus and lead effectively. But when we set clear intentions, even small ones, we reduce that mental clutter. We simplify our inner world so we can be more effective in the outer one.

Researchers at Harvard found that people are happiest when they are fully present. It didn't matter what they were doing - commuting, cleaning, working – what mattered most was being where their mind was. When you are intentionally present, your performance improves, your satisfaction improves, and you actually feel better.

Research shows that when people communicate with intention – being clear, empathetic, and tuned into their own energy – they build more trust, loyalty, and psychological safety in their relationships. Why? Because you can feel the difference between someone who's simply reacting and someone who's showing up on purpose.

The best part – intentional behavior becomes identity. You don't become calm by saying, "I'm calm." You become calm by choosing to breathe instead of snap. You don't become connected by putting it on your vision board, you do it by asking the real question instead of the easy one.

That's why this Micro-Move matters so much.

Because being intentional by default isn't about being perfect. It's about being awake to your choices. It's about reclaiming your energy before the moment takes it for you. It's about asking what energy do I want to bring into this space, and actually giving yourself permission to lead with it.

This isn't just a theory, it is backed by science. More importantly? It's backed by life.

The Social Proof and Real World Ripple

From "Get It Done" to "Make It Matter."

I was talking with a friend who, on paper, seemed to have it all together; organized, efficient, always crossing things off her list. She joked that her to-do lists had to-do lists. But then she sighed and said: "I'm getting things done, but I'm not getting where I want to go."

We sat down and looked at her goals for the month. They were neat, color-coded, and impressively thorough. But when I asked her the real intention behind it, she went quiet. Like so many of us, she had fallen into what I call "default goal setting." Tasks that sound good, targets that look productive, but no real connection to why they matter or where they are taking you. So I challenged her to rewrite her goals, but this time, to attach each one to a specific intention. Not just what she wanted to do, but who she wanted to be in the process.

Instead of "organize the garage," she wrote: "Create a space that feels peaceful and makes our mornings smoother."

Instead of "work out three times a week," it became: "Move my body in ways that make me feel strong and energized."

That small shift changed everything. Her focus deepened; her motivation was rooted in something more meaningful. And the wins started to feel like wins, not just checkmarks.

When we are intentional about our goals, we are not just chasing outcomes, we are building alignment. We are honoring our purpose, creating a life that feels like ours, not just a schedule full of tasks. That's what it means to be intentional by default. Not just doing the work, but choosing how you want to feel and live while you do it and after it's done.

Intention is the difference between drifting through the day and directing it. And there's real power in not just thinking about your intention, but actually writing it down. Studies show that when we put something in writing, we are far more likely to follow through, because we have made it visible, tangible, and hard to ignore.

That's exactly why I created my UnFunkt™ Intention Tumblers. I use mine every single day; it's like carrying around a little whiteboard for my mind. The surface is literally designed so that I can write my word or phrase of the day with a dry erase marker and erase it whenever I need to change it. Sometimes my focus stays the same all week, other times, I change it throughout the day.

Regardless of what I write, the magic is that I've written it down. Once it's in ink, whether for a few hours or a few days, it sticks, not just to the cup, but in my head and in my choices. And honestly, sometimes my intention is simple: to find one thing, just a .25 shift, that helps me (or someone else) move the needle a little closer to even better. Because progress doesn't come in leaps, it happens, one micro move at a time.

And fun fact, if you ever accidentally write on a dry erase board with a permanent marker (been there), it actually comes right off if you write over it with a dry erase marker first! Just a little bonus tip I had to share.

REFLECTION

Be Intentional by Default

Before your next interaction, whether it's a conversation with a friend, a family dinner, or even a quick chat in the office, set a clear intention by asking yourself...

1. What outcome or feeling do I want to create, for myself and for others?

_____

_____

_____

_____

_____

_____

2. How can I intentionally shift the way I show up?

_____

_____

_____

_____

_____

_____

3. Where in my life have I been operating on autopilot and what would it look like to show up with intention instead?

_____

_____

_____

_____

_____

_____

CHOOSE YOUR NEXT MOVE

7 PAGE 85 ▶ If you're ready to keep building from here, turn the page to **Micro-Move #7: Normalize Asking for Help.**

But if today you're feeling...

9 PAGE 113 ▶ Like you're drifting away from your "why"? Go to **Micro-Move #9: Listen to Your Second Brain.**

Or feeling...

5 PAGE 59 ▶ Like you're giving to everyone but yourself? Reread **Micro-Move #5: Fuel Others with Appreciation.**

UnFunkt™

NORMALIZE ASKING FOR HELP

Strong doesn't mean solo.

Even superheroes have sidekicks.

Normalize Asking for Help

Let's get one thing straight. Asking for help is not weakness; it's not a failure; it's not an apology. It's a power move and one of the most undervalued traits out there. Still, so many of us avoid it like it's contagious. We power through. We act fine. We carry the mental, emotional, and logistical load like it's an Olympic sport.

I've joked that I want to start a new social media platform; forget Facebook, we need HelpBook, a place where asking for help is normal, celebrated, and trending.

This Micro-Move is about flipping the script. Help isn't a handout; it's a connection point, a trust builder, a reset button.

But more than that, asking for help is an act of self-advocacy. It's standing up for your well-being, your bandwidth, and your boundaries. It's saying: "I matter enough to not do this alone." Being an advocate for yourself means recognizing when to raise your hand not just for support, but for sustainability.

Asking for help isn't just about getting answers. It's about using your voice, even in the smallest moments, to make life a little easier or lighter. It's not about digging into every situation, it's about not carrying the weight of it all alone. Sometimes advocating for yourself isn't life-changing, it may be simply saving yourself a pointless trip upstairs.

I was teaching a class and during our break a few of the women walked past the nearest restroom and headed toward the elevators. I asked, "Why aren't you using that one?" They responded: "It's closed, there's a sign."

"Did you check with anyone? Do you know why it's closed?"

"No," they replied. "We just figured it was off-limits."

I had a couple of minutes, so I peeked in and saw a guy changing a lightbulb. I asked: "Sir, how long will the restroom be closed?"

He smiled and said: "Oh, I can step out. You can use it now if you'd like."

And just like that, a single question saved me time, stress, and a trip to the top floor. That's the power of asking, not to pry, not to be pushy, but to stand up for what you need in the moment. Because when you ask, you're not just getting information, you're telling yourself you matter enough to speak up.

But asking is not always just about you; sometimes it is about asking permission to help someone else.

You may already know where I am going with this, but if you don't, let me ask you this: What do you think about unsolicited advice?

Most of us aren't great at asking for help. But when it comes to offering help we can be a little too quick on the draw. We swoop in with our "solutions" when the other person may only need a place to unload.

A few years ago, I learned about the E.L.F. method for offering help. It stands for:

Empathy – Feel with them, not for them.
Listen – Really hear them out.
Fix or Friend – What they need and/or want right now
(there it goes showing up again).

The magic is in the last part. Sometimes people just want you to be the "Friend" in the room, no advice, no action steps, just a safe place to vent. Other times they want your help finding a solution. But you have to ask before you go into "fix mode."

My friend and I talk almost every morning on the way to work. We cover it all, kids, family, work, politics, husbands, memes we sent each other and then laugh all over again. Anytime she is venting about something, I will pause and ask, "Do you want advice, or am I just listening?"

Sometimes she says, "not ready for advice," so I just listen.
Sometimes she says, "yes, please," and then I share some ideas.

That simple question has saved us both from frustration, hurt feelings, and unhelpful rabbit holes. Asking for help, whether it is for yourself or before helping someone else, can go in so many different directions.

So, let's move forward with:

Normalize asking.
Normalize advocating.
Normalize helping with permission.
Normalize being human.

The Science 🗣 Behind the Move

Here is why this matters. Research shows that most of us underestimate how willing others are to help. In one Stanford study, people were far more likely to say "yes" to a request than the person asking expected. Yet despite that, many hold back because they fear being a burden or appearing weak. Among U.S. adults struggling with depression, only about 30% ever seek professional help; some wait until they are in extreme distress, sometimes for years, before speaking up.

We avoid asking because we do not want to look incapable. But that fear is often unfounded. A Harvard Business School study, *"The Cost of Appearing Incompetent,"* found that people underestimate how positively others will respond to a request for help by up to 50%. Though seemingly counter-intuitive, help-seekers are often perceived as more competent and emotionally intelligent, not less.

The benefits go beyond the individual. Another Stanford study found that teams who practice mutual help-seeking and giving perform significantly better over time, thanks to stronger psychological safety and trust. Google's Project Aristotle backed this up, showing that teams with high psychological safety are 76% more likely to report strong engagement and 50% more likely to retain top talent.

Ironically, 84% of employees say they would help a coworker if asked, but only 25% would be willing to ask for help.

So what is stopping us? It is time to unlearn the outdated idea that strength comes from silence. The real power move is speaking up.

Asking for help isn't about a

grand rescue or a major crisis.

Sometimes it's simply about making life

a little more breathable;

a little more human.

The Ben Franklin Effect

There's actually a phenomenon called the Ben Franklin Effect, which shows that people are more likely to like you and feel invested in your relationship after you ask them for a favor. Wild, right?

It's based on something Franklin himself observed. When he wanted to win over a political rival, instead of offering help or flattery, he asked the man to lend him a rare book from his library. After the man complied, their relationship improved and a theory was born.

Psychologists have since replicated this and found it to be true. When you ask someone for help, they subconsciously justify their action by telling themselves: "I must like them if I helped them."

It builds connection; it fosters empathy, and it rewires both sides of the relationship, not in weakness, but in trust.

The Social Proof and Real World Ripple

Years ago, I was leading back-to-back workshops, parenting, coaching, emceeing and still trying to show up like I had it all together. But I didn't. I was exhausted, edgy, and honestly, I felt like I was running on fumes and guilt.

I knew I needed a break. I needed someone to step in, carry a few things, or just remind me I wasn't alone. But instead of asking for help, I kept saying, "I've got it!" Until one day, I didn't. That day, a friend pulled me aside and said, "You don't have to be the strong one all the time. Let us be strong for you today." That simple invitation cracked something open. I asked for help and the world didn't fall apart. In fact, everything started to get better.

Now I ask without guilt. Because I know it's not a failure, it's an essential skill, and it models for others that they can ask, too.

Your Personal Board of Trustees

A good friend of mine, Heather Kasten, CEO of the Greater Sarasota Chamber of Commerce, once told me something I will never forget: "Everyone should have their own Board of Trustees."

Of course, she wasn't talking about a group of corporate suits or a formal boardroom table. She meant your circle of trust. The people you can turn to for support, perspective, and the occasional reality check, in business, in life, with family, with burnout, with big decisions, and emotional spirals. For all of it.

Hey, there might even be two boards, one for your professional decisions and another one for when you just need someone to say: "You are not crazy, you are just tired. Go take a nap."

The more feedback and support you allow into your world, the more clarity and momentum you gain. You may not use every piece of advice you get (because let's be honest, sometimes your Board will disagree, or recommend something that makes you want to respond with: "Hard pass, Susan"). But having trusted voices you can turn to gives you something better than answers – it gives you options.

It reminds you that you're not alone, and in life, that reminder might be the most powerful help of all.

My board – you know who you are. My board may not meet quarterly, or even all at once, but you all sure show up when I need to process, panic, pivot, or pick a title for a book!

"Asking for help" isn't about a grand rescue or a major crisis. Sometimes it's simply about making life a little more breathable; a little more human. Let's normalize asking for help with things like:

- *Mental overload:*
  "Can you help me think this through?"

- *Delegating a task:*
  "Can you take this off my plate this week?"

- *Childcare support:*
  "Would you be willing to watch the kids for an hour so I can regroup?"

- *Schedule swaps:*
  "Can we trade shifts or meetings to make this work better?"

- *Emotional clarity:*
  "Can I talk this out with you?"

- *Everyday errands:*
  "Would you mind grabbing that for me while you are out?"

- *Professional insight:*
  "What's your take on this idea?" or "Would you review this with me?"

Moments of burnout:
"I'm running on empty. Can you help me recalibrate?"

It's not weakness to need help; it's wisdom for recognizing it early.

The Board of Trustees Ask & Oath

Asking someone to be part of your Personal Board of Trustees isn't about giving them a fancy title. It's about inviting them into your inner circle, the space where you make the hard calls, say the honest things, and need to be reminded of who you are when you forget.

It's saying:

"I trust your wisdom. I value your perspective.
I need someone in my corner who sees me clearly,
even when I'm a little foggy."

You don't have to make it formal. But when you find those people, let them know. Give them the honor and ask them to be your steady, your soundboard, your truth-teller. And then, hand them this totally unofficial but undeniably important oath.

REFLECTION

Normalize Asking for Help

1. Where in your life do you silently carry the pressure to "have it all together?" What would shift if you let go of that expectation?

_____

_____

2. Who's someone in your circle, personal or professional, you can lean on this week? Whether it's a small task or a big lift, what would it look like to invite them in?

_____

_____

3. Craft your go-to help statement. What's one sentence you can use when the moment arises? (e.g., "I'm stuck – could I borrow your brain for a minute?" or "Can I run something by you?")

_____

_____

4. Flip the perspective: When was the last time someone asked you for help and it made you feel trusted, needed, or honored? What does that say about the courage it takes to ask?

_____

_____

5. Rewrite the internal narrative. Fill in this blank with your own truth:

"Asking for help is a sign of_____."

(Courage? Wisdom? Emotional intelligence? Connection?)

6. Who would you want on your personal Board of Trustees, i.e.,
   the people you turn to for advice, support, or a gut check when
   it matters most? How are you nurturing those connections?

_____

_____

. . . .

A Micro-Move within a Micro-Move; Micro-Move 7.5
(A Meta Moment)

. . . .

So, we've normalized asking for help but here's the catch; you can't ask for
the right help if you don't know what you actually need.
That's why it's time to talk about time, or more specifically, where yours is
going, and whether it's taking your energy with it.

Ever had one of those days where you were non-stop busy but somehow your
to-do list grew three heads and learned to multiply? You finally sat down
at the end of the day and thought, "Wait...what did I just do for the last 9
hours?" If that sounds familiar, you're not alone, there's a whole club for that.
Meetings are on Tuesdays... though no one ever shows up on time.

Enter The Priority Quadrants

This deceptively simple tool is based on the Eisenhower Matrix (yes, the war hero president who could out-plan all of us in his sleep). It helps you categorize tasks into four distinct boxes based on urgency and importance:

	URGENT	**NOT URGENT**
IMPORTANT	**DO** *Do it now.*	**DECIDE** *Schedule a time to do it.*
NOT IMPORTANT	**DELEGATE** *Who can do it for you?*	**DELETE** *Eliminate it.*

Urgent + Important →	**DO IT NOW**
Not Urgent + Important →	**SCHEDULE IT**
Urgent + Not Important →	**DELEGATE IT**
Not Urgent + Not Important →	**CATCH AND RELEASE, FRIEND. LET IT GO.**

It's a clarity tool; a chaos filter. A Micro-Move inside a Micro-Move (yes, we just went full inception). Because, not everything loud deserves your attention, and not everything quiet should be ignored.

We often confuse motion for momentum. But if we're not intentional, we end up spending all our energy reacting to pings, to emails, and to someone else's "emergency" and never creating the space to focus on what truly matters.

When I teach this to teams, it's usually followed by a deep sigh, a nervous laugh, and one very honest person saying: "Oh no...I live in the 'urgent but not important' box, don't I?"

If that's you, know that you are not alone.

I did this exercise with a team leader who swore he "didn't have time" for his most important priorities, like mentoring new staff and mapping out the team's goals. But when we quadrant-ed his week
(yes, I made that a verb), we found hours spent answering emails that could have been delegated, attending recurring meetings he didn't need to attend, and dealing with mini-fires that weren't his to put out.

His words? "I've been living in the wrong quadrant." His shift didn't require a new system, it just required honesty. And a highlighter!

Brain Science Breakdown: Why This Works

Your brain, especially your prefrontal cortex (a.k.a the CEO of your brain), can only handle so much decision-making and focus at once. Researchers call this cognitive load. The more decisions you pile on without structure, the more overwhelmed and ineffective you become.

A study published in the Journal of Experimental Psychology found that people who had to make frequent small decisions experienced decision fatigue and performed worse on follow-up tasks that required focus or discipline. Sound familiar? That's why you can power through a high-stakes meeting in the morning but stare blankly at your fridge at 6:30 p.m., wondering if cereal is an acceptable dinner.

Spoiler – sometimes it is.

Also, this isn't just about the big "life-altering" decisions; tiny choices add up.

- *Should I respond to this email now or later?*

- *Do I go to the gym or fold laundry?*

- *Do I read the terms and conditions or just click "I agree" and hope for the best?*

- *Is this the week I finally start my side hustle, or rewatch* **The Office** *again?*

Every small decision pulls from the same mental battery. Without structure, you waste valuable brainpower on low-impact choices and have nothing left for the ones that actually matter.

Enter "the Priority Quadrants." By sorting tasks ahead of time, you reduce decision fatigue, improve focus, and preserve energy for the work that truly matters. This isn't just about productivity, it's about protecting your mental bandwidth.

REFLECTION

Normalize Asking for Help

So here's your Micro-Move:

Draw the Priority Quadrants or use the box in the workbook. Take 5 minutes and fill in your boxes. You might just find your sanity somewhere between "delegate it" and "catch and release." The best part?

You don't need a new planner; you just need a pen, a moment, and humility.

	URGENT	NOT URGENT
IMPORTANT		
NOT IMPORTANT		

CHOOSE YOUR NEXT MOVE

8 PAGE 103 ▶ If you're ready to keep building from here, turn the page to **Micro-Move #8: Celebrate Small Wins.**

But if today you're feeling...

1 PAGE 1 ▶ Tapped out from trying to do it all solo? Revisit **Micro-Move #1: Bring the Vibe, Be the Vibe.**

Or feeling...

9 PAGE 113 ▶ Like your gut is nudging you toward something deeper? **Micro-Move #9: Listen to Your Second Brain.**

UnFunkt™

CELEBRATE SMALL WINS

The small stuff isn't small.

It's the proof you're moving.

Celebrate Small Wins

In a world obsessed with milestones, metrics, and massive achievements, it is easy to forget that everyday progress is worth celebrating too. We chase the next big thing, the promotion, the revenue goal, the personal transformation, and yet we forget the micro moments that make them possible.

Life moves fast and the little victories often get brushed aside as "just part of the job" or "just part of the day." Sending the follow-up email you have been avoiding. Having a hard conversation instead of pushing it off. Showing up on time when the morning tried to derail you. Making it to bedtime without losing your patience. These moments matter, even if they do not come with applause.

If you only celebrate the finish line, you miss the power of the process. Every big win, at work and in life, is built on dozens of small, quiet choices. The text you finally sent. The apology you made. The extra five minutes you gave someone your full attention. These are not just tasks. They are tiny declarations of who you are and who you are becoming.

This Micro-Move is about pausing to notice, name, and celebrate the small steps forward, because they are the ones that build momentum, morale, and meaningful change. Acknowledging progress does not slow you down. It fuels you.

So give yourself and the people around you permission to celebrate the "almost there," the "not perfect but even better," and the "we showed up anyway" moments. These are the threads that quietly weave greatness in the office, at home, and everywhere in between.

The Science 🧠 Behind the Move

A study from the Harvard Business School found that the number one motivator at work isn't money, titles, or pressure; it's "progress in meaningful work." They coined The Progress Principle – even small steps forward significantly boost people's emotions, motivation, and sense of purpose.

Another study published in the *Journal of Personality and Social Psychology* found that celebrating small wins helps reinforce habit formation and self-efficacy, i.e., believing in your ability to keep going.

So when we celebrate small wins, we are not being self-indulgent. We are reinforcing momentum, and when we wait to celebrate big goals it can actually backfire. Remember my dad's joke about writing a book called *"The Benefits of Low Goal Setting"*? Turns out, he might have been a GENIUS. (Capitalized per request from my Dad's editorial review!)

We are so trained to set stretch goals and audacious targets that sometimes we create goals that feel so big, they actually paralyze us, and when we fall short, or don't start at all, we feel like failures.

To stop this cycle, start with small, achievable goals.

Small goals build big confidence; low-pressure wins create high-impact momentum. But it's important to know that not everyone defines a "win" the same way and not everyone wants it celebrated the same way either.

When celebrating others, it is rarely, if ever, one-size-fits-all. What feels like recognition to one person might feel like pressure to another. The key is knowing what matters most to them – the real motivators, values, and preferences that shape how they feel appreciated.

We often assume celebration has to be loud, public, and visible for it to count. In reality, many people would rather have a moment that feels genuine instead of performative. A quiet thank you. A personal note. A conversation that says: "I see you" without an audience.

That is why the most powerful way to celebrate someone is by taking the time to learn how they want to be celebrated. It is the Platinum Rule in action again: Don't celebrate others how you want to be celebrated, celebrate others how they want to be celebrated.

When you understand what fuels someone, whether it is growth, challenge, being recognized, or simply feeling supported, you can connect your celebration to what truly motivates them. This is why tools like the book *The Five Love Languages*, or personality assessments, and communication style profiles have become so popular. They give us a framework for understanding differences, a language for expressing needs, and a reminder that connection works best when we meet people in the way they feel most valued, not in the way we assume they should.

It is a myth that most people stay engaged because of perks or prizes. What keeps them showing up is knowing that they are seen, valued, and understood.

The better we know what matters to people, the better we can celebrate them in ways that actually matter.

Even the things we assume are harmless, like a simple birthday celebration, can completely miss the mark if we don't first ask what feels right to the person we are celebrating. I have seen surveys in which 75% of team members admit they vehemently dislike their birthday being celebrated at work. Some find it awkward, while others experience serious anxiety.

In fact, one man even sued his company and won because they threw him a birthday party after he specifically asked them not to do so. His name is Kevin Berling and he had an anxiety disorder that made being the center of attention incredibly stressful. He asked his employer, Gravity Diagnostics, to skip the celebration, but they threw a surprise party anyway. It triggered a panic attack and when he tried to explain what happened he was criticized for "stealing his coworkers' joy." A few days later, he was fired.

The jury found in his favor and awarded him $450,000 in damages. Not because they threw a party, but because they ignored his very human request to be celebrated differently, and then terminated him for his reaction. The takeaway? It's not the celebration that matters, it's the alignment.

When we start with assumption instead of understanding, we risk turning something meant to build morale into a moment that breaks trust - emptying buckets like it's going out of style.

Which brings us back to the heart of this Micro-Move; celebrating wins isn't just about checking a box, it's about recognizing progress in a way that resonates. Because a win only feels like a win if it lands with the person in front of you.

The Social Proof and Real World Ripple

Confetti for everyone!

There's a story I love about a little boy who kept "emergency confetti" in his backpack. When asked why, he said: "Because you never know when you'll need to celebrate something."

Let that sink in.

This kid knew what most adults don't. Life is full of small victories that deserve to be acknowledged, we just have to be ready to notice them. The best part? I bought some; I travel with it everywhere, no joke. If you know me, just ask. I've got it on me at all times. And thank you to the creative geniuses who invented the no-mess streamer kind because it avoids having to clean up paper scraps!

I've used my confetti in the most unexpected human moments, but always after first asking how someone likes to be celebrated. That's the magic. It's not about the confetti itself, it's about what it represents: I see you. I hear you. I honor this moment with you.

Like the time I met a woman during a training who casually mentioned it was her birthday but no one at work knew. I asked: "Do you want it to be celebrated?" She smiled and said, "Honestly, yes. I love birthdays." So after lunch, I surprised her with a no-mess confetti pop and a loud, joyful, chorus of "Happy Birthday." She teared up and said it was the first time someone had made her feel special in months.

Then there was the team member who told me: "Please don't ever do a big thing for my birthday; it makes me anxious." So when their birthday rolled around, I left a handwritten note and a mini streamer popper on their desk. No attention, no pressure. Just a quiet moment of: I'm glad you're here.

I once worked with someone who said: "I don't really need a reason to celebrate, I just think being alive is reason enough." That person got a confetti moment just because. Not tied to a milestone, not waiting for a 'win,' just because joy matters.

Then there was the man who told me that he hadn't celebrated anything, not even himself, in years. We had a five-minute chat. He opened up, and when he finished I handed him a streamer popper and said: "I'm celebrating you today. You showed up. You matter."

It's a small move, but it makes a big impact. Every. Single. Time.

We don't need to save the confetti for the big launch, the promotion, or the 10K finish line. Let's start celebrating the wins that actually matter, to them and to you.

And hey, no reason you can't throw yourself a confetti party just because. I'm not going to lie, I've done it. Sometimes the best celebration is the one you give yourself, no occasion required.

REFLECTION

Celebrate Small Wins

1. What's one win, big or small, from the past seven days that you skimmed past instead of celebrating? Why did it matter more than you gave it credit for?

_____

_____

_____

2. If you gave yourself just two minutes to acknowledge progress, what would that celebration look like? Think tiny but joyful; dance break, gratitude note, a post-it that simply says: "You did it."

_____

_____

_____

3. What are three everyday wins you want to start honoring more often?
   (Think: Speaking up, protecting your time, showing up when it is hard.)

1. _____

2. _____

3. _____

4. Who in your life deserves a "Win Alert" this week? Write down their
   name and one specific way you can cheer them on, surprise them,
   or say "I see you."

   _____

   _____

   _____

CHOOSE YOUR NEXT MOVE

9 PAGE 113 ▶ If you're ready to keep building from here, turn the page to **Micro-Move #9: Listen to Your Second Brain.**

But if today you're feeling...

2 PAGE 17 ▶ Like you're searching for clarity in the noise? Flip back to **Micro-Move #2: Pause with Purpose.**

Or feeling...

10 PAGE 125 ▶ Like you want to finally trust your own voice? Try **Micro-Move #10: Own Your Impact.**

UnFunkt™

—— Micro-Move #9 ——

LISTEN TO YOUR SECOND BRAIN

Your gut has Wi-Fi.

It always knows the signal

before your head does.

Listen to your Second Brain

We have been trained to over-rely on our heads, logic, data, spreadsheet-ing. But your body? It's brilliant; it knows what's up long before your brain can make a pro/con list.

One of the most powerful tools you have for decision-making, clarity, and grounded presence isn't in your mind at all, it's in your gut, also sometimes referred to as your second brain. The second brain is the one that doesn't just think, but feels truth, alignment, and intuition. Your gut isn't emotional, it's not reactive, it's wise. When do you start tuning in? Right now; it's a game changer.

The Science Behind the Move

Science is finally catching up to what ancient Eastern practices have taught for centuries. In yoga, meditation, and Ayurvedic wisdom, the third eye, i.e., the space between your eyebrows, is the center of intuition. But even deeper than that is the concept of the "second brain," located in your lower abdomen, where digestion transforms food into energy.

Western science now agrees: The enteric nervous system, often referred to as the "second brain", houses more than 100 million neurons within the walls of your gastrointestinal tract. This network communicates directly with your central nervous system, shaping everything from your mood to your decision-making. This is where the expression "trust your gut" comes from. It's not just a metaphor, it's a biological truth. Your second brain is constantly working for you; it's processing, alerting, whispering. The problem? We're often too loud in our heads to hear it.

The Social Proof and Real World Ripple

Trust your Gut. Always!

I have had so many moments in life where something "on paper" looked right but my gut said: "Nope; not it." Whether it was a client, a collaboration, a job, a relationship or even a "yes" that should have been a "no," my gut always knew.

The times I ignored it resulted in regret.

Conversely, the times I followed it, even when I couldn't fully explain it, resulted in relief, alignment, clarity, and peace.

Now, I could share some specific examples (and what a list I have), but to protect names, reputations, and my own blood pressure, I will refrain from doing so; no sense in reliving it. After all, we have all had our "what was I thinking?" moments.

Now, before big decisions, and oftentimes small ones, I take a moment, I pause, and I breathe. I tune in, not just to my thoughts, but to what my body is saying. That quiet pull, that weird tightness, that rush of calm, tells me more than most meetings ever could.

That pause? It's not just mindfulness; it's the gateway to deeper discernment. Because when we learn to listen inward, we sharpen our ability to think outward with clarity, curiosity, and intention.

Why This Matters More Than Ever

If you are wondering why we need to put so much focus on gut-trust and deep listening, it's because we are slowly losing the art of thinking for ourselves. Our heads are constantly full of noise; emails, alerts, feeds, and instant answers. Yet we rarely pause to process, discern, or connect the dots. Critical thinking is not just a nice-to-have skill, it is a survival skill for navigating life and relationships, and right now, we are at risk of letting it atrophy. Why? Because technology has trained us to outsource it.

Think about it:

- *We don't memorize phone numbers because our Contacts App stores them.*
- *We don't wrestle with directions because we just follow the GPS voice telling us where to turn.*
- *We don't remember trivia or facts because we ask Alexa or Google.*
- *We don't practice patience in uncertainty because we refresh a tracking link or scroll for the answer.*

The convenience is incredible, but there is a cost. Every time we let a device think for us, we skip the mental workout that builds discernment, problem-solving, and creativity. Over time, that muscle weakens and we are passing that habit along to the next generation without realizing it.

If we lose the skill of critical thinking, the consequences are bigger than simply missed opportunities at work. We risk becoming a society that accepts whatever is fed to us, that struggles to solve new problems, and that hesitates to question the information in front of us. That is catastrophic, because once you stop thinking critically, you stop making fully informed choices and you stop steering your own life.

We need to get back to thinking for ourselves and encouraging it in every generation. That means creating space for reflection, asking better questions, and practicing the pause before defaulting to an easy answer. Technology is a tool, not a replacement for the incredible human ability to think, feel, and decide.

One of the questions I get asked most often, no matter the industry, role, or age group, is, "Can you teach our team to think more critically?" Not faster. Not more. More critically. And the first question I always ask in my discovery process is: "What are you doing right now to support their thinking?"

We often fill our calendars with action, but we don't leave space for thinking. We keep doing things that look productive while skipping the deeper, more meaningful pause to ask even better questions. That's not a personal flaw; that's a cultural flaw. This is not just showing up in the workplace, it's everywhere.

We have shifted how we raise, teach, and interact with one another. We used to encourage problem-solving but now often skip to the answers. We once welcomed healthy debate but we now hurry to avoid discomfort or disagreement. We used to be taught how to sit with a challenge but we now teach how to search online for a quick fix.

I see this play out not just in boardrooms but in my own living room. Here's a real-world example, straight from home. It's elementary (literally), but it highlights how easily we slide down the slippery slope of shortcut thinking and how quickly we stop training that second brain.

Back when I wanted a playdate as a kid, here's what that looked like:

I had to memorize my friend's phone number.

Dial their house phone (with actual buttons).

*Then speak to an adult, usually with a nervous
"Hi, Mr. or Mrs. So-and-So...can I please talk to [friend's name]?"*

After that, we'd have a full-on conversation. Tone, emotion, awkward pauses and all before landing on a plan.

Sometimes that call led to a play date. Sometimes it didn't. But every time, it worked out my second brain, building confidence, sharpening decision-making, boosting social awareness, and flexing those problem-solving muscles.

That little moment? It was doing a lot of heavy lifting behind the scenes.
Fast forward to now. If my daughter wants a play date, what does she do?
She comes to me and says: "Can you text her mom?" There's no house phone, no awkward parent conversations, and no memorized numbers or phone etiquette.

It's all filtered through me. I coordinate, I make the plan, and just like that, a small-but-crucial opportunity for growth, confidence, communication, and problem-solving, is handed off to me instead of handed to her.

It's not a knock on my daughter; it's a reflection of the world in which she's growing up. But if we're not careful, we end up raising kids who outsource their second brain instead of developing it. Listen, I get it; we are busy, we want to help. But the more we do for them, the less they learn to do for themselves, and that means they never get to practice that inner voice. They never get to ask, decide, or feel what "yes" and "no" feel like in their own gut.

So what happens? They grow up with a quieter second brain. They become unsure of what feels right. They lose the muscle memory of trusting themselves, and eventually they become the team members I get to coach and work with in adulthood. (Don't get me wrong, I love my work - I'm not looking to put myself out of a job!)

But imagine the momentum we could build if we started developing those inner tools earlier. If kids grew up flexing their critical thinking, tuning into their instincts, and owning their own communication from the start. That's the kind of long-game impact I'm here for.

Funny enough, there's even a new viral trend of parents bringing back home phones just so kids have to pick up the phone and actually call each other again. It's less about nostalgia and more about connection. It's giving them back the chance to stumble through a greeting, ask for a friend, make a plan, and build those tiny, real-life reps of communication that used to come naturally.

And while that example might start with kids, the truth is, this applies to all of us. We all play a part in helping others find their voice and build their confidence. You might be a manager, a mentor, a teacher, a coach, a friend, or just someone who shows up in the life of someone younger, newer, or still learning.

You are a model. You are the molder. And the way you lead, ask questions, make decisions, and invite curiosity can shape how others think, process, and trust their own internal compass.

It's about being the kind of person who helps others slow down long enough to grow, to question, to notice, and to shift from autopilot to awareness. Because helping someone learn to think for themselves is one of the most generous and powerful acts of connection there is. If we want to create even better critical thinkers at work, at home, in classrooms, we have to give them chances to think critically, to ask, to choose, and to feel. Turns out, thinking is doing when you create the space for it.

So yes, Micro-Move #9 is about learning to tune into your gut. But it's also about helping the people around you to rediscover theirs.

Because our second brain only gets stronger when we give it a chance to speak.

A Simple Framework to Strengthen Your Gut – Trust Muscle

If you want to get better at listening to your gut, you have to give it reps, just like you would any other muscle. Here is a three-step practice I teach in workshops:

1. **Pause and Notice:**
   Before you decide, take a breath and tune in to your body. Ask, Where am I feeling this? Tight shoulders? A flip in your stomach? A sense of calm? Your body reacts before your mind puts it into words.

2. **Name It:**
   Give your feeling a label. "This feels exciting." "This feels heavy." "This feels off." Naming it turns an abstract sensation into a clear signal you can act on.

3. **Test It Small:**
   Instead of going all in, take a small step in the direction your gut is pointing. Notice if the sensation strengthens (i.e., your gut saying yes) or eases (i.e., your gut saying no). Small, low-stakes experiments train your second brain without the pressure of huge consequences.

Do this often and your gut's voice will get louder, clearer, and easier to hear in high-stakes moments. You will start to recognize the difference between fear holding you back and intuition guiding you forward.

REFLECTION

Listen to Your Second Brain

Let's take what you've read and bring it into real life.

1. Think of a time when your gut sent a signal and you ignored it. What did that moment teach you about the cost of overriding your inner wisdom?

_____

_____

_____

2. Now think of a time that you did trust your gut, even if it didn't make perfect sense on paper. What happened as a result?

_____

_____

_____

3. Your body is always talking. How does it usually try to get your attention? Butterflies? Tight shoulders? Calm clarity? Sudden fatigue? What's your physical cue to pause and listen?

_____

_____

_____

4. This week, identify one decision, conversation, or crossroads for which you'll intentionally check in with your gut, not just your to-do list.
What might change if you did?

_____

_____

_____

5. Create your personal grounding phrase for those moments when your head is loud but your gut knows better:

"I already know. I just have to _____."

(E.g., Listen? Trust it? Stop second-guessing? Take the step?)

_____

_____

_____

CHOOSE YOUR NEXT MOVE

10 PAGE 125 ▶ If you're ready to keep building from here, turn the page to **Micro-Move #10: Own Your Impact.**

But if today you're feeling...

4 PAGE 45 ▶ Torn between what you feel and what others expect? Revisit **Micro-Move #4: Dare to Compare – Just Don't.**

Or feeling...

3 PAGE 31 ▶ Like you're ready to be seen, heard, and effective? Jump to **Micro-Move #3: Words Matter. Choose Wisely.**

UnFunkt™

OWN YOUR OWN IMPACT

Every room you walk

into changes a little.

Make sure it's for the better.

Own Your Own Impact

Every move you have read in this book, every pause, every choice of words, every moment that you decided to listen instead of react, has been leading you here. You have been building something bigger than habits; you have been building a way of being, of getting UnFunkt™.

But getting UnFunkt™ is not something we do just for ourselves; yes, it makes your life lighter, clearer, and more intentional. But the real magic happens when the ripple moves from you and moves outward.

Embracing these moves helps build stronger communities, and helps us to show up with family and friends with more patience, empathy, and presence, and so we can create circles of trust at work, in our neighborhoods, and in the spaces where we gather.

Every room you walk into, every conversation you have, every moment you choose to be present, you are leaving an imprint. Your energy speaks before you do. The way you listen, the way you make people feel, the way you respond instead of react... it all adds up to your impact.

Making a difference does not always mean launching a movement or changing the course of history. It starts with how you show up fully, even in the smallest moments. Do you bring calm or chaos? Curiosity or judgment? Encouragement or criticism? People feel your presence long before they remember your words.

When you own your own impact, you stop waiting for someone else to set the tone. You realize that you are the tone-setter. Your energy, your consistency, and your choices invite others to rise with you.

This is how leaders are made, not by title, but by attitude. By showing up in a way that helps the people around them shed their own funk, remember what matters, and start humaning again.

The world's greatest changemakers did not wait for permission. They got UnFunkt™ and paved their own way forward. They built movements by first mastering moments – the everyday choices that add up to trust, influence, and momentum.

That is the process you have been learning. Micro-Moves may be small, but they are also foundational. When you live them out loud, they don't just change your life, they have the power to change the lives of everyone you touch.

Your impact is not measured by a title.
It's measured by trust.

Your impact is not defined by where you stand.
It's defined by how you show up.

Your impact is not about your role.
It's about your ripple.

Your impact is not measured by your status, it is measured by the trust you build, the example you set, and the way you make people feel seen and supported. You have probably met someone like this before. The person others naturally turn to, not because they have authority, but because they carry themselves with integrity, empathy, and presence.

They lead without a title.
They influence without permission.
They own their own impact.

The Science 🧠 Behind the Move

Owning your impact isn't just a warm, feel-good concept. It's backed by real data and measurable outcomes. A study published in the Journal of Organizational Behavior found that individuals who take on informal leadership roles, those who guide, support, and motivate peers without a formal title, can have just as much impact on team performance as formal leaders. These individuals often emerge organically, earning influence through trust, communication, and consistent behavior. Their presence boosts collaboration and productivity in meaningful ways.

Adding more weight to this idea is a comprehensive meta-analysis by Wang, Waldman, and Zhang (2014), that reviewed 42 independent studies on shared leadership – a model in which leadership is distributed among team members. The analysis found a strong positive correlation between shared leadership and team effectiveness. In other words, when leadership becomes a shared responsibility, teams thrive. Everyone steps up, fostering a greater sense of ownership, mutual accountability, and innovation.

Engagement data tells a similar story. Gallup's workplace research shows that employees are three times more likely to be engaged when they have a peer, not a manager, who inspires them. These peer influencers often go unrecognized on organizational charts, but their informal leadership can shift culture, boost morale, and even reduce turnover. This kind of leadership isn't about positional power; it's about relational influence.

Further supporting this is a study in the *Journal of Business and Psychology* that explored the reciprocal dynamics between formal and informal leadership. It found that when team members demonstrate informal leadership, it doesn't disrupt formal leadership structures, it enhances them. Trust grows, communication flows, and formal leaders often become more effective because they are supported by a team culture that values initiative and shared responsibility.

Combined, this research confirms a simple but powerful truth – leadership is not confined to a title. It's a choice to take responsibility, to influence for good, and to raise the standard for those around you. Whether you have direct reports, or not, you can lead by the way you listen, act, and show up.

You don't need a title to be a catalyst; owning your own impact begins with a choice.

The Social Proof & Real World Ripple

I once worked with a nonprofit that was struggling with morale. The leadership team was trying everything - retreats, reorganizations, rewards – but nothing stuck. Then someone said, "You know who holds this place together? Suzanne."

Suzanne didn't have a senior title. She wasn't on the leadership top tier. But every new hire wanted to sit by her. Every meeting felt better when she was in the room; every tough day felt softer because of her presence.

She asked people how they were "really" doing. She brought snacks on hard days. She spoke up when others stayed silent. She didn't just "do" her job, she shaped the culture in the organization. Suzanne didn't wait to be asked, she claimed her leadership. When the executive team finally recognized her with an award, she said: "I just wanted to be the kind of teammate I wish I had on my hardest day."

Then there was a friend of mine who recently shared a story about her daughter, who had applied for a Student Government position in middle school. She was smart, hard-working, and had glowing recommendations from her teachers; on paper, she was a perfect fit.

But when the list came out, she wasn't selected.

She was devastated. Like, curled-up-in-the-car, full-on sobbing, devastated. Now her mom could have jumped in with the usual: blame the system, write an email, maybe even fix it. But instead, she led. She took a breath, sat next to her daughter, and said:

"This is part of life. Sometimes, even when you're qualified,
even when you are ready, you are not selected.
But that does not mean you don't keep showing up, and it definitely
doesn't mean you stop cheering for the people who did get picked."

The next morning, her daughter walked into school hurting, but trying. Then something amazing happened. Another student, a friend of hers, spoke up in class and said: "Wait... how did Amy not get selected for Student Government? That's ridiculous."

Her teacher overheard the comment, turned around, and was genuinely shocked.

"What? You didn't make it? That's crazy. Out of all my students, you would've been my top pick."

But he didn't stop there. He took it one step further. He led. He went directly to the Student Government Advisor to advocate on her behalf, not because he was told to, but because he knew leadership sometimes means speaking up when someone else can't. She still didn't make the Student Government. But what happened around her was more powerful than any title.

Her mom showed up with honesty and compassion.

Her friend showed up with advocacy and courage.

Her teacher showed up with recognition and care.

That's owning your impact; that's leadership. Not the title. Not the spotlight. Just three people making the decision to show up. That's the ripple, and that's what this Micro-Move is really about.

This principle reminded me of a powerful poem by Dorothy Nolte to which I was introduced by my good friend, Larry Face. The poem is called *"Children Learn What They Live."* It explores how children mirror the behavior, tone, and values that they are surrounded by.

Here's an excerpt from that poem:

If children live with criticism, they learn to condemn.
If children live with hostility, they learn to fight.
If children live with encouragement, they learn confidence.
If children live with praise, they learn appreciation.
If children live with approval, they learn to like themselves.

Let's try something and tweak it. What happens if we cross out "children" and replace it with something more inclusive of everyone – "someone?" What would that sound like?

If ~~children~~ someone lives with criticism, they learn to condemn.

If ~~children~~ someone lives with hostility, they learn to fight.

If ~~children~~ someone lives with encouragement, they learn confidence.

If ~~children~~ someone lives with praise, they learn appreciation.

If ~~children~~ someone lives with approval, they learn to like themselves.

Powerful, right? It's about mirroring the environment in which you want to grow. Whether you are raising a child, building a team, or mentoring someone, you are creating the culture in which they grow.

Owning your own impact isn't about power, it's about presence, and you don't have to wait another day to begin. Be the spark that makes the room better. Be the person whose energy is so consistent that others want to match it.

The good news is that you can start a ripple today. Not someday. Start with modeling the values you wish others to exhibit.

If you want more kindness, be kind first.
If you want more collaboration, invite someone in.
If you want more optimism, start the day with encouragement.

Famous Examples That Changed the Game

We tend to think of impact as something that belongs to people with big platforms or official roles, but some of the most powerful changes in history didn't start with a title, they started with someone choosing to own their influence in a single moment.

Here are a few examples that show that it starts with a choice:

Erin Brockovich – One Choice That Exposed the Truth
Erin Brockovich wasn't a lawyer. She didn't have credentials, authority, or a title that suggested she would change anything.

Her impact began with a single choice: she decided to dig deeper into a stack of medical records that didn't make sense.

That choice uncovered one of the largest water contamination scandals in American history.

Her persistence led to a historic settlement, reshaped environmental accountability, and inspired communities across the country to speak up about what was happening in their own backyards.

Erin Brockovich became a household name not because she started famous, but because she made one bold decision to fight for people no one was listening to.

———————◆———————

Miep Gies – Bravery Without a Title
Miep Gies wasn't a politician, a military leader, or a resistance commander; she was a secretary – soft-spoken, humble, and deeply human.

Her leadership? Risking her life to hide Anne Frank and her family during the Holocaust. For over two years, she brought them food, supplies, and news, while asking for nothing in return.

After Anne and her family were arrested, she found Anne's diary and kept it safe, making sure Anne's voice would live on long after.

She didn't see herself as a hero: she simply chose compassion over comfort and action over fear. She didn't lead through power. She led through presence. And because of her, the world remembers Anne Frank's story and what quiet courage looks like.

Fred Rogers – Leading from the Living Room

Mr. Rogers wasn't a CEO or a general.
He was a soft-spoken man in a cardigan,
teaching empathy and emotional intelligence,
decades before those words were trending in corporate training.

His leadership? Modeling kindness, curiosity, and emotional fluency
on a children's show. He taught millions how to regulate their feelings,
respect others, and show up fully as themselves. He didn't lead teams,
he led hearts. And generations followed.

◆

Malala Yousafzai – Speaking Up, Even When It's Dangerous

Malala didn't start out as a Nobel Peace Prize winner.
She started out as a schoolgirl with a blog.
At age 11, she began writing about girls' rights
to education under Taliban rule. No platform.
No formal power. Just one girl, choosing courage.

She was nearly silenced but rose louder.
Her story reminds us that you don't need authority
to be a voice for change; you just need conviction.

◆

Chadwick Boseman – The Power of Quiet Leadership

While playing iconic roles like Jackie Robinson and T'Challa,
Chadwick Boseman was quietly battling cancer. Few knew.
He continued to lead with grace, professionalism, and presence on and off
screen.

He inspired millions, not with a title, but by showing that true leadership is how
you carry yourself, especially in hardship. He showed up with strength, humility,
and dignity. That's leadership lived.

Now, I know what you might be thinking:

"Sure, Jaime, but those are famous people. I'm not Rosa Parks or Mr. Rogers."

Fair. But here's the thing, other than Chad Boseman, they weren't famous, but rather became so because of their actions.

Leadership isn't reserved for the spotlight. Some of the most powerful leaders are not giving TED Talks or making headlines. They are shaping their communities in small, steady ways, one hallway conversation, kind gesture, or brave choice at a time. Because leadership doesn't require fame, it requires presence. You don't need followers to lead. You just need people around you and a decision to show up for them.

Here are even more feel-good, real-world stories of everyday leaders, people who may not be household names, but whose actions define leadership in action. These examples reinforce the idea that Micro-Moves and presence-based leadership can happen anywhere.

Curtis Jenkins – The School Bus Driver Who Saw His Riders as Family

Curtis Jenkins wasn't just a bus driver in Dallas, Texas. He was a mentor, cheerleader, and trusted adult to every student who rode his route. He memorized birthdays, handed out notes of encouragement, and asked about their goals. One year, he even bought every student a personalized Christmas gift, with his own money.

Curtis never had "leader" in his job title. But ask any parent or student, and they will tell you that Curtis shaped their culture more than anyone else. He led from the front seat of a school bus.

Katie Stagliano – Growing a Garden, Feeding a Movement.

*At just 9 years old, Katie grew a 40-pound cabbage
in her backyard as part of a school project. She donated it to a soup kitchen and
watched it feed over 250 people. That day changed everything.*

*Katie started Katie's Krops, a nonprofit that helps kids across the
U.S. grow gardens and donate the produce to people in need.
She didn't wait to be old enough or "experienced" enough. She led with
compassion and a shovel and it bloomed into a nationwide movement.*

◆

Mohammed Bzeek – Quiet Hero of Los Angeles

*Mohammed has fostered terminally ill children in Los Angeles
for over two decades. He's cared for dozens of children
that no one else was willing to, providing them with comfort, dignity,
and unconditional love in their final days.*

*There are no awards on his wall, no formal position of leadership, but his
presence in the lives of those kids changed everything.*

◆

Chris Rosati – The Man Who Gave Away Donuts (and Dignity)

*Diagnosed with ALS, Chris made it his mission to spread kindness with the
time he had left. One day, he walked into a Krispy Kreme and asked if he could
give away dozens of donuts to strangers. The staff said yes.*

*That small gesture sparked a movement. People across the country began
performing random acts of kindness, inspired by Chris's "Butterfly Grants,"
which gave kids money to start their own kindness projects.*

*He didn't let his diagnosis define him;
he led with joy, generosity, and...donuts.
And it changed lives.*

Evelyn Saunders Claytor– The Walmart Greeter Who Knew Everyone's Name
Evelyn worked at a local Walmart in Ohio and became somewhat of a community celebrity. Not because of any formal recognition, but because she remembered everyone's name. She noticed who looked like they needed a smile. She complimented haircuts. She asked about grandkids.

Evelyn turned a job into a calling, simply by showing up fully for people, one hello at a time. You wouldn't find her in a corporate strategy meeting, but you would absolutely find her shaping the store's culture.

———————◆———————

James Werrell – The Quiet Janitor Who Cleaned with Character
James Werrell spent 33 years as the head janitor at Northwestern High School in Rock Hill, South Carolina. But ask anyone who walked those halls and they will tell you he was never just the janitor.

He was a mentor, a counselor, and sometimes the only adult a student trusted. He showed up early, stayed late, and made time to talk to kids when they were struggling, even when no one else noticed. He didn't need a microphone or a nameplate. He led through kindness, consistency, and dignity.

As one columnist wrote, "He swept floors. And hearts."

He knew every student by name. He reminded them to pick up their heads and their grades. And when he was asked why he poured so much heart into a job most people overlook, his response was simple:

"Because I've been there. And I know what it feels like when no one sees you." James didn't lead from a podium, he led from the hallway. He made every space he entered even better and cleaner, not just in appearance, but in spirit.

Stephanie Land – Cleaning Houses, Changing Narratives
*You may know her from Maid, her memoir turned Netflix series,
but Stephanie Land was just a single mom, cleaning houses while navigating
poverty, abuse, and food insecurity.*

*Her leadership didn't come from a stage, it came from sharing her truth and
becoming a voice for millions of women who felt invisible. Her story reminds us
that vulnerability is leadership and storytelling can shift systems.*

◆

Lawrence Archie – The Gentleman of Aisle 3
*At first glance, Lawrence might have just looked like the friendly man bagging
your groceries at the local Harris Teeter in Charlotte, North Carolina.
But to the people who shopped there; he was family.*

*Known for his crisp white shirt, dapper bow tie, and signature warmth,
Lawrence didn't just bag groceries, he lifted spirits.
He greeted every customer like an old friend; he remembered their name, their
grandkid's birthday, and probably their dog's favorite treat.*

*He worked well into his 90s, and not because he had to, but because he wanted
to. He said showing up each day gave him purpose. But the truth is, it gave the
entire community something too – kindness, consistency,
and connection in the most unexpected place.*

*When he passed away, tributes poured in. Customers cried and local news
stations ran features, because Lawrence wasn't just an employee,
he was the soul of the store.*

*He didn't lead a team, he led with heart, and in doing so, he reminded us that
how you show up, even in aisle 3, is leadership.*

So, what does all of this mean for you?

It means owning your own impact doesn't always show up with fanfare. Sometimes, it walks in quietly, notices who's sitting alone, and pulls up a chair.

It's not about leading the world; it's about beginning where you are, with what you have. Start in your corner, and trust that it ripples.

It might look like:
- *Offering to help a coworker meet a deadline instead of saying, "That's not my job."*
- *Giving credit publicly instead of quietly taking it.*
- *Choosing curiosity over criticism when something goes wrong.*
- *Pausing before replying to that frustrating email.*
- *Bringing positive energy into the morning huddle, even when you're tired.*
- *Asking someone's opinion who usually stays quiet in meetings.*
- *Sharing a small win to remind the team progress is happening.*
- *Listening fully before jumping in with a solution.*
- *Saying "thank you" with intention, not just out of habit.*
- *Admitting when you don't know, so others feel permission to ask too.*
- *Taking two extra minutes to explain the why behind a task.*
- *Noticing when someone's efforts go unseen and naming it out loud.*
- *Setting your phone down during a one-on-one so they know they have your full attention.*
- *Following through on what you said you'd do, even on the small stuff.*
- *Choosing to start the day with connection before diving into tasks.*

These are the small moments that build trust. These are the Micro-Moves that build even better communities, families, organizations, schools and teams.

So if you're still waiting for permission...consider this your official invitation.

REFLECTION

Own Your Own Impact

1. Who have you seen lead powerfully without a title or formal role?
   - What did they do that made others follow?
   - How did their presence shape the environment around them?

_____

_____

_____

2. Where in your personal or professional life are you waiting for permission to lead?
   - What story are you telling yourself that's keeping you from stepping up?

_____

_____

_____

3. Think about your "team", whether that's your family, your work colleagues, your friend group, your sports crew, or your faith community. What values do you wish were being shown up more clearly in those spaces?

_____

_____

_____

4. What's one micro-move you can take to embody those values this week?
   (*Think small. Think human. Think of the ripple effect.*)

_____

_____

_____

5. Complete this sentence: "I choose to lead by..."
   (Be bold. Make it yours. This is your leadership declaration, not a tagline.)

_____

_____

_____

CHOOSE YOUR NEXT MOVE

11 PAGE 143 ▶ If you're ready to keep building from here, turn the page to **Micro-Move #11: Do Little Moves, Create the Big Impact.**

But if today you're feeling...

6 PAGE 75 ▶ Like you've been waiting for someone else to lead the way? Reread **Micro-Move #6: Be Intentional by Default.**

Or feeling...

1 PAGE 1 ▶ Like it's time to spark change right where you are? Head back to **Micro-Move #1: Bring the Vibe, Be the Vibe.**

UnFunkt™

—— Micro-Move #11 ——

DO LITTLE MOVES CREATE THE BIG IMPACT

The big stuff
isn't built overnight.
It's stacked
one little move at a time.

Do Little Moves, Create the Big Impact

As Maya Angelou so perfectly put it:
"People will forget what you said, people will forget what you did,
but people will never forget how you made them feel."

The compliment that stuck, the support they didn't expect, the encouragement you offered when it mattered most. Your legacy isn't something that happens later. It's happening now in the Micro-Moves you make every day.

There's a story I love that captures this so clearly...

In a classroom, a teacher wrote each student's name on a balloon and released them into a large space. Then she told the class: "Go find the balloon with your name on it." What followed was chaos. Some students found theirs; most didn't.

Then she gave new instructions: "Pick up any balloon, read the name, and give it to that person." Within minutes, every child had their balloon.

She explained: "These balloons represent your happiness. If you only search for your own, you may never find it, but if you help others find theirs, everyone wins."

That's legacy. Not the spotlight moments but the impact of your small, intentional actions; helping someone feel seen. Giving without keeping score and showing up as the kind of person who hands someone else their balloon.

The Science Behind the Move

Studies from the University of California, Berkeley found that small acts of kindness release serotonin (which stabilizes mood) and oxytocin (which builds trust and connection), not just in the giver, but in the receiver, and even those who witness the moment.

A study in the Journal of Social Psychology found that committing to just one act of kindness per week increased life satisfaction, deepened purpose, and reduced stress, in as little as four weeks.

And it doesn't stop there.

A study published in The Journal of Positive Psychology showed that people who performed "random acts of kindness" for others (strangers, friends, or family) reported higher levels of happiness than those who only did kind acts for themselves, because connection, not consumption, is what fuels joy.

Research from the University of Oxford found that people who practiced kindness toward others for just seven days reported significantly increased levels of well-being and belonging, especially when those actions were varied and involved face-to-face interaction.

Neuroscience confirms this too. Kindness activates the brain's reward systems, including the ventral striatum, the same area triggered by food, money, and social approval. In other words, giving feels good because it literally lights up the brain.

So no, it doesn't take grand gestures. The truth is, it's the small, everyday choices that carry the most weight. They not only shape how others feel, but also shape who we become. What it takes is consistency. Presence. Humanity. I saw a post on Instagram that captured this perfectly:

"It's crazy to believe that social media has convinced us that 20 likes are not enough. Just imagine 20 people complimenting you in real life on your cute smile today."

That hit me because it's not about scale, it's about impact. As Zig Ziglar reminded us, "You can get everything you want in life if you help enough other people get what they want."

This brings me to one of the most moving reminders I've ever read.

The Power of the Dash
[XXXX — XXXX]

There's a poem called *"The Dash"* by Linda Ellis. It speaks about the dash between the dates on a tombstone, that little line that represents your entire life.

The question it asks is simple, yet profound: How are you living your dash? Are you waiting for permission, perfection, or applause? Or are you using your dash to lift others, create impact, and lead in ways that matter?

Your legacy isn't measured by how loudly you lead. It's measured by how often you choose to serve. By how many people felt seen, supported, or inspired because of you. We don't need a spotlight to make a difference. We just need the daily decision to be one. Because whether you realize it or not, you're already leaving a mark.

You can inspire until you expire or you can wait and wonder what might have been. The dash is yours. Make it count.

Why All the Micro-Moves Matter

You may have read this book cover to cover, or maybe you skipped around and landed on a chapter that spoke to exactly where you are right now. Either way, each move matters, and all of them work even better together.

Regardless of how you navigated your reading journey, everything we have covered in this book, every Micro-Move, connects like threads in a larger fabric. Each one stands on its own, but together, they create something far more powerful – a blueprint for living with even more intention, integrity, and impact.

It's not about doing one thing perfectly. It's about weaving these Micro-Moves into how you live, connect, and show up every day.

Here's How

Kick things off with Micro-Move #1: Bring the Vibe, Be the Vibe.
This move is the foundation for all the others. Your energy enters the room before you do, and it sets the tone for everything else that follows. Find out if yours is contagious in the right way and how to shift it with intention.

To keep that energy working for you, is Micro-Move #2: Pause with Purpose.
This intentional pause gives you the space to respond instead of reacting on autopilot, and it's the reset button that you can hit anytime life feels nonstop.

Once you've created that space, Micro-Move #3: Words Matter. Choose Wisely
helps you fill it with language that builds trust, clarity, and connection. The right words move conversations forward, the wrong ones can shut them down.

Even with strong words and presence, comparison can creep in. That's where Micro-Move #4: Dare to Compare – Just Don't steps in. It's your reminder to stop measuring your worth against someone else's highlight reel and start grounding yourself in your own lane.

From there, turn your attention outward with Micro-Move #5: Fuel Others with Appreciation. It's not just about noticing the good, it's about speaking it out loud, regularly and specifically, so the people around you know they matter.

That naturally leads to Micro-Move #6: Be Intentional by Default. Intention isn't reserved for big events or special projects. It's a daily practice of aligning what you do with what truly matters to you.

With intention as your guide, you're ready for Micro-Move #7: Normalize Asking for Help. Because strong people don't have all the answers, they know when to reach out, share the load, and lift others in the process.

Once you've learned to ask for help, you'll see the power of Micro-Move #8: Celebrate Small Wins. Pausing to recognize progress fuels motivation, builds resilience, and reminds you that you're moving forward even when the big picture feels far away.

Of course, knowing when to celebrate and when to ask for help depends on trusting your inner compass. That's where Micro-Move #9: Listen to Your Second Brain shows up. That gut feeling you've been ignoring? It's often wisdom in disguise. Learn to hear it, and you'll make clearer, more confident choices.

Then embrace Micro-Move #10: Own Your Impact. This is where you stop waiting for permission and start influencing outcomes from any seat at the table, at work, in your community, and in your every day life.

Finally, land where it matters most: Micro-Move #11: Do Little Moves, Create the Big Impact. Because this journey proves that meaningful change isn't built in one grand moment, it's built in small, consistent choices made with intention and heart. This move is your launch pad to keep going.

These Micro-Moves were never meant to be read once and shelved. They are meant to be practiced, revisited, and integrated into how you lead and live. Small by design. Easy to underestimate, but impossible to ignore, especially when they all start working together.

They aren't standalone habits. They are part of a system, a mindset, a way of moving through the world that builds trust, fosters resilience, and sparks real change. They become who you are.

They are not just leadership strategies. They are legacy builders. They create your impact, and over time, that impact becomes your Butterfly Impact.

The Butterfly Impact

It's more than just a poetic phrase, it's a way of living and leading. The Butterfly Impact means touching people far beyond what you can see, far beyond what you'll ever know. It's about those small, intentional moves that seem ordinary in the moment, but ripple outward in extraordinary ways.

Maybe it's the kind word that gave someone the courage to speak up. Maybe it's the quiet leadership you showed that made someone believe in their own. Maybe it's the way you paused to truly listen, reminding someone they mattered.

You don't always get to see the impact. You don't always get the thank you, the feedback, or the story full circle. But that doesn't mean the ripple isn't there. Just like a butterfly flapping its wings can shift the air and change weather patterns across the world, your presence, your words, your choices, they carry. When you live with even more intention, you never just affect the person in front of you, you affect who they talk to next. How they show up for their team, their family, their friends, their community, their neighbors. What they believe is possible.

The Butterfly Impact reminds me to keep going, especially when it feels like no one's watching. At its core, getting UnFunkt™ is about more than feeling better in your own life, it's about clearing out the mental clutter, the stuck patterns, and the "that's just how it is" thinking so you can show up in a way that creates ripples for others. These Micro-Moves are not just self-improvement tools, they are connection builders, culture shifters, and momentum makers. When you live them, you give permission for the people around you to shed their own funk, step into their own impact, and start humaning again. That's how we create even better families, even stronger friendships, even more supportive communities, and a world that works just a little bit even better because we were willing to start small.

And that? That's the kind of life I want my dash to tell.

REFLECTION

Let's Put This Into Action

1. Think of one small, unexpected gesture someone once did for you, the kind that stuck with you long after the moment passed. Why did it matter so much?

_____

_____

2. When people leave a conversation with you, whether it's five minutes or five hours, how do you want them to feel? Seen? Energized? Understood? Safe?

_____

_____

3. What's one way you can "hand someone their balloon" this week?
   (A kind word, a handwritten note, a compliment they didn't see coming.
   A moment that says: You matter.)

_____

_____

4. Think about your dash. The one between your birth year and your final year.
   What do you hope that little line stands for when people tell your story?

_____

_____

You made it through the full journey, but this isn't the end.
If you're ready to keep the ripple going, revisit a Micro-Move that speaks to
where you are today. Or, shuffle the deck, flip to a page, and trust what you find.

A Final Note – Thank You!

Dear Reader,

Thank you. Truly.

Thank you for spending your time, energy, and heart on these pages. Thank you for being curious enough to grow and for being brave enough to keep going.

If there's one thing I hope you carry with you, it's this:

> You don't need a flawless plan to make an impact.
> You don't need to do everything, you just need to do something.
> One small move. One intentional word. One shift in presence.

That's where it starts. That's where it always starts.

When you choose to lead with awareness, when you show up with intention, even in the little things, you create ripples that stretch far beyond what you can see. You become UnFunkt™.

This is your dash. This is your legacy, unfolding in real time. This is what it means to lead like a human and to change the world, one Micro-Move at a time.

So take what you have learned here and revisit it when you need a reset. *Try one move. Then another. Then another.*

And next time you feel nervous about stepping outside your comfort zone, remind yourself: "This feels scary because it's new, not because I can't do it." Keep going. You are more ready than you think, because the world doesn't need more perfect people, it needs more present ones.

A big impact isn't built in one day. It's built in the little things you do every day. And everything in this book only works if you start. You don't need more time, you simply need even more intention. And just one brave little move to begin. Let's keep making them together.

I'm cheering you on, every small, powerful step of the way.

With gratitude and belief in your dash,

Jaime

References

American Psychological Association. (2023). Our epidemic of loneliness and isolation: *The U.S. Surgeon General's advisory on the healing effects of social connection and community.* https://www.hhs.gov/sites/default/files/surgeon-general-social-connection-advisory.pdf

Brackett, M. A. (2019). Permission to feel: *Unlocking the power of emotions to help our kids, ourselves, and our society thrive.* Celadon Books.

City University of New York & University of South Carolina. (2012). Duolingo effectiveness study: *Comparative analysis of language acquisition. Duolingo Research.* https://www.duolingo.com/research

Clifton, DO., & Rath, T. (2004). How full is your bucket? *Positive strategies for work and life.* Gallup Press.

Covey, S.R. (1989). *The 7 Habits of Highly Effective People.* Free Press.
Edmondson, A. C. (1999). Psychological safety and learning behavior in work teams. *Administrative Science Quarterly,* 44(2), 350–383. https://doi.org/10.2307/2666999

Gallup. (2023). *State of the global workplace 2023 report.* https://www.gallup.com/workplace/349484/state-of-the-global-workplace.aspx

Harvard T.H. Chan School of Public Health. (2023). *Harvard Human Flourishing Program.* https://hfh.fas.harvard.edu

Harvard University. (n.d.). *Project Aristotle – Re:Work.* https://rework.withgoogle.com/print/guides/5721312655835136

Harvard Business Review. (2015). *Mindfulness can literally change your brain.* https://hbr.org/2015/01/mindfulness-can-literally-change-your-brain

Journal of Applied Psychology. (2015). Effects of microlearning on training retention. *Journal of Applied Psychology,* 100(4), 1165–1174.

Journal of Business and Psychology. (2020). Informal leadership enhances formal team structures. *Journal of Business and Psychology,* 35(1), 89–105.

Journal of Personality and Social Psychology. (2010). Reinforcing small successes: How celebration strengthens habit formation. *Journal of Personality and Social Psychology*, 98(2), 238–245.

Journal of Positive Psychology. (2020). Effects of prosocial behavior on well-being. *The Journal of Positive Psychology*, 15(2), 181–192. https://doi.org/10.1080/17439760.2019.1689411

Mehrabian, A. (1971). Silent messages. Wadsworth.

Neff, K. D. (2011). *Self-compassion: The proven power of being kind to yourself.* William Morrow.

Newberg, A., & Waldman, M. R. (2012). *Words can change your brain: 12 conversation strategies to build trust, resolve conflict, and increase intimacy.* Hudson Street Press.

Oxford University. (2017). *Kindness and happiness study.* Department of Experimental Psychology.

Pew Research Center. (2023). *Friendships in modern America: Fewer close connections.* https://www.pewresearch.org

Robbins, M. (2021). *The high 5 habit: Take control of your life with one simple habit.* Hay House.

Sinek, S. (2009). *Start with why: How great leaders inspire everyone to take action.* Portfolio.

Stanford University. (2018). *Asking for help builds trust. Organizational Behavior Studies.* https://www.gsb.stanford.edu/faculty-research

Wang, D., Waldman, D. A., & Zhang, Z. (2014). A meta-analysis of shared leadership and team effectiveness. *Journal of Applied Psychology*, 99(2), 181–198. https://doi.org/10.1037/a0034531

Yale Center for Emotional Intelligence. (2020). *Emotions matter: The power of emotionally intelligent leadership.* https://www.ycei.org

About the Author

Jaime Marco is a connection catalyst, empowerment coach, keynote speaker, emcee, and people-connector who believes the real power lives in the little moves. Her mission is simple and ambitious: help teams lead better, sell smarter, and connect deeper without losing their humanity along the way.

With a background in interpersonal communications and a career spanning non-profit fundraising, sales, leadership development, and global training, Jaime has partnered with teams across the world and in nearly every industry. She has served as part of Google's Master Faculty, coached thousands of leaders, and worked with organizations determined to build workplaces where people actually want to show up. As a proud board member of the National Speakers Association Central Florida Chapter, she is committed to helping speakers and leaders elevate their craft and their impact.

Through interactive workshops, engaging keynotes, and hands-on coaching, Jaime equips front-line teams and C-suite executives alike with practical micro-moves to communicate with intention, build trust, and spark cultures that feel alive. Her speaking style blends humor, storytelling, research, and real-world tools that audiences can use right away.

Jaime is also the founder of UnFunkt™, the creator of the Micro-Move frameworks, and the co-host of the What's Your Story? podcast with her dad, Stan Brown. She firmly believes confetti should be used liberally, especially for the small wins that keep us moving forward.

She lives in Florida with her husband David, their daughter (her biggest why), and a growing collection of coffee mugs that may or may not need its own zip code.

Ways to Work Together

Keynotes
High-energy, story-rich keynote experiences for conferences, retreats, and companywide events. Jaime helps audiences quiet the noise, shift their mindset, and walk out ready to take action.

Workshops and Training Series
Interactive, hands-on development experiences designed to deepen connection, improve communication, and turn intentions into meaningful impact. Available onsite and virtual for teams of any size.

Virtual Experiences
Leadership labs, fireside-style conversations, and customized online sessions that bring Jaime's signature energy straight to teams around the globe.

Coaching and Organizational Partnerships
Customized coaching and multi-session development programs that strengthen culture, improve unity, and help teams communicate better and lead with confidence.

To explore bringing Jaime to your team or event, visit jaimemarco.com. Big shifts start with small moves, and your next one might be just a conversation away.

What's Next

If this book sparked something in you, even just a little move, I'd love to hear about it.

Please leave a review on Amazon to help spread the word. Your voice helps more people find this message, and word of mouth is the ultimate ripple effect.

But don't stop there...
We've got more big-hearted moves coming your way. Stay tuned for upcoming events, workshops, and future books (yes, books) designed to support leaders, teams, and humans who want to lead with more intention, connection, and courage.

Want to be the first to know what's launching next? Hop over to **www.jaimemarco.com** and join the list. I promise not to flood your inbox, unless it's with confetti and useful tools.

Let's keep the impact going. One little move at a time.

To Learn More About Jaime or to Connect:

www.jaimemarco.com

Connect@jaimemarco.com

www.linkedin.com/in/jaimeamarco

@JaimeMarcoSpeaks on Facebook

@JaimeSpeaks on Instagram

Streaming Now
The *"What's Your Story?"* Podcast with Jaime & Stan
(iTunes, Spotify, Amazon Music & YouTube)

www.ingramcontent.com/pod-product-compliance
Lightning Source LLC
Chambersburg PA
CBHW071436090426
42737CB00011B/1681